The BUSINESS of BOOKS

The de Bellaigue Report

Foreword by Clive Bradley

HUTCHINSON

London Melbourne Sydney Auckland Johannesburg

Hutchinson & Co. (Publishers) Ltd

An imprint of the Hutchinson Publishing Group

17-21 Conway Street, London W1P 6JD

Hutchinson Publishing Group (Australia) Pty Ltd
PO Box 496, 16-22 Church Street, Hawthorne, Melbourne,
Victoria 3122

Hutchinson Group (NZ) Ltd
32-34 View Road, PO Box 40-086, Glenfield, Auckland 10

Hutchinson Group (SA) Pty Ltd
PO Box 337, Bergvlei 2012, South Africa

First published 1984
© 1984 Eric de Bellaigue

Printed and bound in Great Britain by
Anchor Brendon Limited, Tiptree, Essex

British Library Cataloguing in Publication Data

De Bellaigue, Eric
   The business of books
   1. Publishers and publishing - Great Britain - Statistics
   I. Title
   338.4'70705'0941   Z323

ISBN 0 09 158211 3

The Business of Books

Contents

Foreword

Introduction

Foreword

by Clive Bradley, Chief Executive, The Publishers Association

A clear understanding of financial performance and market trends is essential to effective management in any industry. When that industry is as subject to extraordinary external pressures as British book publishing is - currency parities affecting the important export markets, government pressures on public spending in education and libraries, competition (and stimulation) in the market place from new media, pervasive changes in the use of leisure time, changes in retailing practice, and the whims of public taste - that knowledge becomes absolutely crucial to management planning, growth, and service to the market.

The sheer complexity of British book publishing has always made detailed information on the industry difficult to obtain. Over the past few years, however, the industry has made a determined and consistent effort to collect and analyse valuable information about itself. The Government's Business Statistics Office, acting on the stimulus to Government statistics given by Sir Claus Moser, is now providing reasonably consistent series of publishing turnover, flawed by base changes in 1978 and again in 1980, but now divided into sensible publishing categories. A more detailed Publishers Association analysis based on sixty major publishers, including details of unit sales, returns, and export markets has been undertaken since 1977. A book price component has been added to the Retail Price Index, though based on a lamentably inadequate sample. The Whitaker's database, from which British Books in Print is published in cumulative supplements, monthly microfiche, and annual volumes, and the British National Bibliography, both increasingly available on-line, provide a growing bank of information on what is published in all categories of books, with edition and catalogue details.

The measurement of financial management performance has been harder to achieve - only a handful of firms support the highly valuable Inter-Firm Comparison, sponsored by the Publishers Association, with its detailed hierarchy of performance ratios - but commercial comparisons based on filed accounts from Inter Company Comparison and Jordans now include rigorous data on all parts of the book trade. And another commercial company, Euromonitor, has undertaken a study of consumer book buying and reading habits for a number of years, which is producing increasingly valuable data on trends in the marketplace. The PA hopes to commence a similar, more detailed series shortly, and its Book Marketing Council has undertaken important market research into reasons for lost sales and into impulse buying.

So the book trade is now relatively well documented, and Eric de Bellaigue's study, bringing together some of the more vital information from many of these series, and applying to it the trained mind of a financial analyst, not only for the UK but for the USA and Australia as well, is a very important contribution to our understanding of our business, as well as a useful reference book. He has applied sensible and consistent conventions to the interpretation of the figures, so that the work has great authority. It is, too, of great general interest in helping to assess the innate strength of an industry which illuminates both public and private life.

Clive Bradley

Introduction

The Business of Books is a challenging title. It is particularly so for somebody who is outside publishing - though I have been a fascinated observer of the industry for over fifteen years.

In the present report, two things have been attempted. Firstly, in looking at the subject I became conscious of the difficulties of securing consistent statistical information on the industry. It occurred to me, therefore, that it might be doing a service to readers to assemble what information could be obtained and to point up some of the strengths and weaknesses of the various statistical series available. And since the future is of greater interest than the past, I have included population projections and a number of outside forecasts.

While there are quite a few existing studies on UK book publishing, most of them confine themselves to this country. In the present study, the factual material extends beyond the UK to include Australia and the United States. This aspect of the report is aimed, therefore, to provide publishers and others interested in the industry with a brief statistical reference tool.

The second objective has been to offer some response to the title The Business of Books. The chapter entitled The American Challenge considers the specific threat posed to traditional UK markets by US publishers. The future role of the UK publisher in Australia is the subject of another chapter, while the section on the USA considers the different approaches open to UK firms in that market. The chapter on paperbacks is an attempt to trace likely trends, based on both UK and US experience, while that entitled Production views the subject very much from the standpoint of a UK firm.

The largest section, amounting to about one third of the report, is concerned with the United Kingdom, with the heaviest emphasis on distribution. One of the concluding chapters covers briefly some aspects relevant to book publishing of the development of the newer technologies.

Throughout the non-statistical sections of the study, considerable reliance has been placed on contacts within the industry. Much of the narrative consists, in fact, of commentaries on individual companies' actions and objectives. In this connection I felt that it would add interest to the work for such companies to be named. Also, my thinking was that these sections might have some value to other publishers in so far as the examples supplied could spark ideas relevant to their own operations. Under such circumstances, anonymous reference would deprive the material of practical bite.

I am immensely indebted to all those whom I importuned with my questions, whether it be in Australia, the USA or the UK and am very appreciative of the tremendous amount of time and help that was given me. My chief thanks, however, are due to London Weekend Television and the Hutchinson Group whose initial interest led to the preparation of a study which forms the basis of this report.

WORLD POPULATION BACKCLOTH

Any attempt at considering the prospects for the UK publishing trade must start with a brief analysis of population trends. And since UK publishing retains a heavy overseas bias, these trends need to cover a wide range of countries. In the following tables a preliminary attempt has been made to describe the demographic framework within which UK publishers will be operating during the next ten years or so.

Table 1

World Population Trends

(millions)	1969-70	1975-76	1979-80	1985-86	1989-90	1995-96
WORLD TOTAL	3,670.3	4,098.6	4,396.4	4,801.4	5,249.3	5,711.2
North America	226.2	238.2	246.7	257.5	268.1	278.1
Latin America	278.7	327.3	365.9	421.9	479.0	538.9
EEC	260.4	267.9	270.7	272.1	274.6	277.3
Other W Europe	73.6	77.1	79.1	81.5	84.1	85.8
East Europe*	368.4	387.7	400.0	417.5	432.7	449.8
Africa**	453.6	538.0	604.2	692.1	791.4	897.9
Asia	1,990.1	2,240.9	2,407.0	2,634.7	2,893.8	3,156.2
Oceania	19.3	21.6	22.7	24.1	25.5	27.1

*Including the USSR   **Including Mideast
Note: Minor discrepancies are due to rounding
Sources: UNESCO 1981 Yearbook; Predicasts

In the decade to 1980, world population grew by 726.1m and in the decade to 1990 the increase is expected to rise to 852.9m. If the world is broken down into developed countries and developing countries, the following pattern (Table 2) emerges. (The totals differ slightly from those in Table 1.).

In the decade to 1980, developed countries experienced a rise of 89.2m in their aggregate population and within that total the 0-24-year-olds advanced by 3.1m. In the same decade, developing countries saw their population expand by 649.1m and within that overall total the 0-24-year-olds increased by 364.1m.

Looking ahead to the decade to 1990, the developed countries are expected to witness a population expansion of 85.2m and within that total a contraction in the 0-24-year-olds of 4.8m. In the same period, developing countries are forecast to see their aggregate population rise by a further 775.6m and, within that total, the 0-24-year-olds rise by 341.2m.

1

Table 2

World Population Trends in Developed/Developing Countries

(millions)	1969-70	1975-76	1979-80	1985-86	1989-90
World, of which	3,676.8	4,033.3	4,415.0	4,830.2	5,275.7
aged 0-24	2,034.3	2,230.1	2,401.4	2,567.9	2,737.8
Developed, of which	1,074.6	1,122.0	1,163.8	1,206.9	1,249.0
aged 0-24	468.3	474.6	471.4	468.1	466.6
Developing, of which	2,602.1	2,911.3	3,251.2	3,623.3	4,026.8
aged 0-24	1,566.0	1,755.5	1,930.1	2,100.0	2,271.3

Source: UNESCO 1981 Yearbook

In very broad terms, these statistics serve to highlight the way in which population trends will be a decreasing source of dynamism within the developed countries - a rise of 85.2m in the 1980s compared with a rise of 89.2m in the 1970s and, of particular importance to those industries that cater to the young, an actual decline in the 0-24-year-olds of 4.8m against a rise of 3.1m.

Within developing countries, the pace of population growth is also expected to slow down, but the absolute numbers remain vast.

Reference to Table 1 highlights the fact that the rate of growth will remain extremely high in Africa and Latin America. It is also of some interest to note that the 0-24-year-olds will account for 44 per cent of the overall growth in population, against 56 per cent in the previous decade, a sign of a more 'mature' population pyramid. From the point of view of suppliers to many of these markets, the main limiting factor naturally remains purchasing power.

In later sections of this report, the population projections of selected countries will be presented.

THE UNITED KINGDOM

1. UK Population Projections

Between 1971 and 1981 the population of the United Kingdom rose by 505,000. In the decade to 1991, the population is forecast to rise by 1,172,000. In contrast, therefore, to the projections for developed countries discussed earlier, overall population movements in the United Kingdom will be somewhat more favourable to growth in the 1990s than they were in the 1980s. The contrast will be heightened, moreover, by the fact that in the 1976-81 period the UK population virtually stood still.

Table 3

UK Population Trends

(thousands)	1971	1976	1981	1986	1991	1996
TOTAL	55,515	55,959	56,020	56,416	57,192	57,939
0-19	17,220	17,081	16,304	15,614	15,574	16,244
0-4	4,505	3,738	3,465	3,997	4,440	4,417
5-9	4,670	4,446	3,717	3,438	3,967	4,411
10-14	4,213	4,652	4,445	3,710	3,430	3,959
15-19	3,832	4,245	4,677	4,469	3,737	3,457
20-64	30,989	30,955	31,396	32,395	33,097	33,295
20-34	11,106	11,677	12,239	12,671	13,257	12,732
35-44	6,500	6,343	6,729	7,581	7,739	7,757
45-64	13,383	12,935	12,428	12,143	12,101	12,806
65+	7,306	7,925	8,320	8,407	8,521	8,400

Source: Annual Abstract of Statistics, 1982, CSO

In Table 3 the population has been divided into three broad categories, the 0-19-year-olds corresponding roughly to the age groups that go to form the educational establishment, the 20-64 band that comprises the labour force and the 65+ band that consists of the retired. The absolute changes in the five-year periods are shown in Table 4.

3

Table 4

UK Population Changes 1971 to 1991

(thousands)	1971 to 1976	1976 to 1981	(1971 to 1981)	1981 to 1986	1986 to 1991	(1981 to 1991)
Total	+444	+61	+505	+396	+776	+1,172
0-19	-139	-777	-916	-690	-40	-730
0-4	-767	-273	-1,040	+532	+443	+975
5-9	-224	-729	-953	-279	+529	+250
10-14	+439	-207	+232	-735	-280	-1,015
15-19	+413	+432	+845	-208	-732	-940
20-64	-34	+441	+407	+999	+702	+1,701
20-34	+571	+562	+1,133	+432	+586	+1,018
35-44	-157	+386	+229	+852	+158	+1,010
45-64	-448	-507	-955	-285	-42	-327
65+	+619	+395	+1,014	+87	+114	+201

Source: Derived from Annual Abstract of Statistics, 1982, CSO

Clearly, within the figures of total UK population, there have been and will continue to be major divergent trends.

Table 4 illustrates the fact that the population decline in the 0-19 age brackets that characterized the 1971-81 period will persist in 1981-86; by the mid-1980s a plateau will have been established with virtually no change in the overall totals taking place between 1986 and 1991. Looking somewhat closer at the 0-19 breakdown, it is clear that the substantial decline in the 5-9-year-olds, amounting to 729,000 or 16.4 per cent that took place in 1976-81 period will work its way through to the 10-14-year-olds in 1981-86 and the 15-19-year-olds between 1986 and 1991. The only area of population growth within the 'educational establishment' (as defined earlier) is estimated to be among the 0-4-year-olds. This will also show up in the 5-9-year-olds between 1986 and 1991; in that period the projected population increase among the 0-9-year-olds amounts to 972,000, or 13 per cent of those two combined bands.

The wide category of 20-64-year-olds is expected to account for virtually all of the population growth projected in the 1980s (outside of the areas that have already been singled out in the earlier analysis of the 0-19-year-olds). And within this group, the greatest growth in absolute terms will come among the 35-44-year-olds in the period 1981-86, and the 20-34-year-olds between 1986 and 1991. Some further but modest expansion is anticipated in the 65+ band.

Relating these population projections to the book publishing industry, the following points may be made:

(a) In the 1980s, the population changes are on the whole negative as far as suppliers to the 'educational establishment' are concerned. This is particularly true of the 10-19 age bracket; the second half of the decade should, however, see a useful advance in the 5-9-year-olds.

(b) The 20-34 age bracket, having advanced by a little over 1 million in the 1970s is expected to rise by almost the same amount in the 1980s. Other things being equal, this should provide a helpful environment for products relevant to household formation.

(c) The first half of the 1980s is witnessing a big absolute rise in the number of 35-44-year-olds amounting to 852,000, which in percentage terms represents a sizeable increase of 12½ per cent. The development of hobbies is traditionally regarded as a characteristic of those who fall within this age bracket.

(d) Growth will have largely gone out of the 65+ (retired population) band in the 1980s. This follows a significant expansion in the 1970s; to take an example outside of publishing, this was something that the travel firm Saga Holidays was clever enough to exploit through marketing tours that catered specifically to the needs of the elderly.

2. UK Book Reading and Buying Habits

Before looking at the statistical material available on the UK book industry, it may be useful to glance at what is known as the sociology of book buying and reading, a vast subject, which is only lightly touched upon here (Table 5).

A breakdown of readers by class reveals a not-surprising connection between more intensive reading the higher one moves up the socio-economic grid: within the AB socio-economic grouping, 67 per cent of those interviewed in a survey undertaken by Euromonitor in 1983 were currently reading a book, against 38 per cent and 37 per cent for the C2 and DE groups respectively.

If, however, these percentages are related to the population figures, also divided according to class, the weighted readership percentages show that the semi-skilled and unskilled manual group (DE) forms numerically the largest book reading market with 30 per cent of the total. The middle and upper group (AB) is little more than three-fifths the size at 19 per cent. The Euromonitor survey goes on to analyse the source of the books that are being read (Table 6).

5

Table 5

Readership Patterns in the UK - 1983

(% now reading)	Readership	Weighted Readership
AB (Middle and upper)	67	19
C1 (Lower middle)	53	25
C2 (Skilled manual)	38	26
DE (Semi-skilled and unskilled manual)	37	30
TOTAL	45	100

Source: The Book Report, 1983, Euromonitor Publications

While purchases form the biggest segment at 37 per cent, they are only slightly greater than the 34 per cent shown for public library borrowings. The public library system is discussed briefly in a later section; suffice it to say that the evidence of Table 6 highlights its importance in the UK, with women heavier users than men. The 3 per cent 'don't knows' is somewhat alarming: one must hope that it simply reflects genuine forgetfulness.

Table 6

Sources of Books Currently Being Read

(per cent)	Men	Women	Total
Library	32	36	34
Bought	40	34	37
Borrowed	11	19	15
Gift	10	6	8
In home	3	3	3
Don't know	3	3	3
	100	100	100

Note: Discrepancies are due to rounding
Source: The Book Report, 1983, Euromonitor Publications

If one focuses on the books bought (Table 7), the survey entitled Impulse Buying of Books which the Book Marketing Council published in July 1982, is of considerable interest. The survey itself was based on contacts with a representative sample of 60 bookshops and 50 CTNs (confectionery, tobacco and newsagents shops) and involved interviews with 2,482 shop users. Of the bookshop users, as many as 72 per cent made no purchase at all. One way of looking at this statistic is to see in it a measure of the scope that exists for more effective marketing (from the publisher downwards) and salesmanship.

Of the 28 per cent that did buy in bookshops, 48 per cent acquired the book(s) they had planned to purchase and 52 per cent bought on impulse. In the CTNs planned purchases only accounted for 25 per cent of the total and impulse purchases for as much as 75 per cent. The size of these two percentages has in turn clear implications for the importance of the packaging of books as well as of their display. Within impulse purchases, remainders accounted for 8 per cent in bookshops and up to 16 per cent in CTNs.

Table 7

Patterns of Book Buying

(per cent)	Bookshops	CTNs
Planned purchases	48	25
Impulse purchases, of which	52	75
paperback purchases	72	NA
remainder purchases	8	16

Source: Impulse Buying of Books, The Book Marketing Council, July 1982.

In terms of format 72 per cent of bookshop impulse purchases consisted of paperbacks, with CTNs showing a higher proportion (not quantified). The great majority of all remainders were hardbacks.

To conclude this brief section, Table 8 presents a breakdown of the adult reading market which encapsulates admirably the complex motives that readers have and the rough consequences this has on patterns of book purchases and book borrowings. It is taken from a paper presented by Dr Peter Mann in March 1982.

Table 8

Adult Reading

ADULT READING

WORK   LEISURE

Utilitarian	Extrinsic	Social	Intrinsic	Personal
Work books	Home manuals	Non-fiction	Fiction	Distraction
Texts	& Reference	History	'Literature'	Mystery
Manuals	Cookery	Biography	'The novel'	Romance
Reference	Cars	Travel		Detective
School books	Hobbies			Thriller
Academic texts	Guides			Western

Buy to have at hand
for reference

Status-conferring
reading

No status

Borrow from library
and
may buy personal copy

Reviewed

Throw-away

Challenging ideas

Sold in 'real'
bookshops

Paperbacks
Mass sales

Great deal of borrowing

Source: Libraries and the Reading Habit, Peter Mann, Public Libraries Group of the Library Association, 1982

3. UK Consumer Expenditure on Books

In Table 9 consumer expenditure on books during the course of the last ten years is presented in terms of both current prices and constant prices. Also shown are the figures for consumer spending on other forms of print, alcohol, tobacco and entertainment.

Table 9

Consumers' Expenditure

		1971 £m	1976 £m	1981 £m	1971 to 1976 %	1976 to 1981 %	1971 to 1981 %
Books	(A)	104	236	562	+127	+138	+440
	(B)	181	201	224	+11	+11	+24
Newspapers	(A)	319	638	1,279	+100	+100	+301
	(B)	604	548	524	-9	-4	-13
Magazines	(A)	109	182	375	+67	+106	+244
	(B)	203	162	168	-20	+4	-17
Beer	(A)	1,526	3,282	6,385	+115	+95	+318
	(B)	2,372	2,738	2,575	+15	-6	+9
Spirits	(A)	670	1,491	2,899	+123	+94	+333
	(B)	933	1,312	1,464	+41	+12	+57
Wine	(A)	397	986	2,150	+148	+118	+442
	(B)	632	888	1,158	+41	+30	+83
Tobacco	(A)	1,691	3,107	5,553	+84	+79	+228
	(B)	2,605	2,653	2,492	+18	-6	-4
Cinema	(A)	63	81	142	+29	+75	+125
	(B)	109	67	54	-39	-19	-50
Radio/TV	(A)	364	878	1,501	+141	+71	+312
	(B)	446	838	972	+88	+16	+118
Other enter- tainment	(A)	222	517	1,338	+133	+159	+503
	(B)	341	463	519	+36	+12	+52
TOTAL	(A)	35,599	74,850	151,042	+110	+102	+324
	(B)	59,724	64,707	71,762	+8	+11	+20

(A) At current prices   (B) At constant prices
Source: National Income and Expenditure, 1982 edition, CSO

The first point that emerges is that expenditure on books has been much better sustained than has been the case with the other two broad categories of print, newspapers and magazines. Indeed, over the decade, there was an actual contraction in real terms of 13 per cent and 17 per cent in newspapers and magazines, while books expanded by 24 per cent.

A closer look at the other areas of expenditure that have been chosen for their leisure of quasi-leisure characteristics highlights the boom in radio and TV (much of it rental) and in consumption of wine, which can almost be taken as a proxy for the growth of travel. The losers have been the consumer equivalent of the 'smoke stack' industrial world, beer, tobacco, and the cinema. Within these broad classifications, the performance of a long-established product such as books, which has not benefited from the novelty factor that has boosted some other goods and services, can be seen as having been thoroughly respectable. This is best appreciated perhaps in Table 10 which shows the share of total consumer expenditure accounted for by the different sectors.

Table 10

The Share of Consumer Expenditure taken by Selected Items

	1971		1976		1981	
(per cent)	(A)	(B)	(A)	(B)	(A)	(B)
TOTAL	100	100	100	100	100	100
of which,						
books	0.29	0.30	0.32	0.31	0.37	0.31
newspapers	0.90	1.01	0.85	0.85	0.85	0.73
magazines	0.31	0.34	0.24	0.25	0.25	0.23
beer	4.29	3.97	4.38	2.69	4.23	2.04
spirits	1.88	1.56	1.99	2.03	1.92	2.07
wine	1.12	1.06	1.32	1.37	1.42	1.61
tobacco	4.75	4.36	4.15	4.10	3.68	3.47
cinema	0.18	0.18	0.11	0.10	0.09	0.08
radio/TV	1.02	0.75	1.17	1.30	0.99	1.35
other entertainment	0.62	0.57	0.69	0.72	0.89	0.72

(A) At current prices   (B) At constant prices
Source: Derived from National Income and Expenditure, 1982 edition, CSO

In current price and constant price terms, books have more than held their own. In some areas, such as radio/TV, the sharp reductions in prices achieved as a result of technological advance are seen in a slight <u>fall</u> in the share in current prices of such spending between 1971 and 1981, at the same time as a near doubling occurred in real (constant price) terms.

While it has to be accepted that broad aggregates of the kind presented in the National Income and Expenditure statistics have their limitations when it comes to trying to visualize the prospects for a minor component such as books, and even more so the prospects of specific sectors within the book trade, the following comments do seem justified:

(a) The ten years covered do not provide evidence that books, taking UK sales as a whole, are losing their position in consumers' spending habits.

(b) This decade has, moreover, witnessed the development of major new claims on consumer discretionary income, which makes the performance of books all the more commendable.

(c) It seems likely that books have in the past managed to avoid confronting the UK consumer with harsh alternatives - of the kind that makes him have to choose, for example, between either a can of beer or a bottle of wine.

(d) These broad aggregates relate only to consumer spending in the UK on books. That is to say, they include spending on imported books and exclude exports from the UK and the development by UK publishers of indigenous publishing in overseas markets.

(e) As will be seen later in this report, however, other statistics are not as comforting to the book trade as are those in the national accounts.

4. UK Book Publishing Statistics

The most widely used statistics summarizing the performance of the UK publishing industry are those presented in Table 11; they show publishers' receipts on home and export sales. That 1981 home sales of £703m should have been well ahead of consumer expenditure on books (Table 9) of £562m is explained by the fact that government expenditure on books is included in the book publishing statistics and does not form part of consumer spending.

The figures themselves are derived from the Business Monitor statistics and then subjected to a grossing up factor by the Publishers Association so as to take care of the firms that have been excluded from the Government statistics by reason of their small size. The employment threshold has in the past been changed - from 6 to 25 in 1978 and again altered in 1980; this determines inclusion or exclusion from the raw Business Monitor figures. The Publishers Association has sought to adjust the Business Monitor figures for the changes in the reporting threshold. Inevitably, however, comparability from one year to another has become somewhat suspect.

On exports, the figures are understated: since 1980 no allowance is made for the sale abroad of books by UK retailers and wholesalers; the sums are important and an export proportion some five percentage points higher than that shown is probably called for. While the statistics are difficult to interpret, there has undoubtedly been a contraction in the proportion accounted for by exports since a peak of 39.1 per cent achieved in 1977. One influence has been the partial replacement of exports to UK publishers' overseas subsidiaries by locally published titles.

Table 11

UK Book Publishing Statistics

| Year | Turnover Statistics (a) | | | | Titles Issued in the UK | | | |
	Home	Export (£million)	TOTAL	Export as % total	New Books	Other (b)	TOTAL	Price per book
1983					38,980	12,091	51,071	NA
1982	764	336	1,100	30.5	37,947	10,360	48,307	11.45
1981	735	342	1,077	31.8	33,696	9,387	43,083	10.04
1980	664	312	976	32.0	37,382	10,776	48,158	9.09
1979	561	283	844	33.5	32,854	9,086	41,940	7.86
1978	476	275	751	36.6	29,530	9,236	38,766	7.34
1977	398	255	653	39.1	27,684	8,638	36,322	6.58
1976	347	216	563	38.4	26,207	8,227	34,434	5.85
1975	302	167	469	35.6	27,247	8,361	35,608	4.68
1974	240	143	384	37.2	24,342	7,852	32,194	3.66
1973	198	115	314	36.6	25,698	9,556	35,254	3.24
1972	187	101	288	35.1	24,654	8,486	33,140	3.21

Annual Rates of Growth - Per Cent Change

	Home	Export	TOTAL		New	Other	TOTAL	Price
1972-82	+15.1	+12.8	+14.3		+4.4	+2.0	+3.8	+13.6
1977-82	+13.9	+ 5.6	+11.0		+6.5	+3.7	+5.8	+11.7
1972-77	+16.3	+20.3	+17.8		+2.3	+0.4	+1.8	+15.4

(a) Grossed up estimates of publishers' receipts made by the Publishers Association to account for publishers not contributing to the Business Monitor enquiry
(b) Reprints and new editions
Sources: The Publishers Association, The Bookseller, Business Monitor

The Bookseller has courageously put a value on all these qualifications/uncertainties and calculates in its September 11, 1982 issue that total UK book publishing turnover in 1981 really came to £1,200m, within which home sales are estimated at £750m and export sales at £450m. This indicates an export percentage of 37.5 per cent.

The number of titles issued (Table 11) forms a somewhat contentious statistical series, being a compilation of the weekly lists published by The Bookseller. The main feature in the period covered is the comparatively modest rise in the number of titles issued each year in the five years 1972-77, followed by an explosion of publishing activity through to

Table 12

Breakdown of Publishers' Turnover at Current Prices

Year	Bibles*	School textbks	Tech & scient	Fiction Lit Classics	Childrens	Other	TOTAL
(£thousands)							
1982	12,163	115,186	179,202	190,214	63,199	217,353	777,317
1981	12,304	125,118	165,907	182,627	61,951	216,240	764,147
1980	11,780	112,821	134,622	162,212	56,998	214,405	692,838
1979	9,618	97,437	100,250	138,038	55,255	197,251	597,849
1978	10,692	89,851	87,485	132,266	46,968	168,139	535,401
1977	10,337	79,237	76,900	109,884	40,107	135,725	452,190
1976	9,665	67,199	68,526	95,654	38,445	113,707	393,196
1975	7,059	55,324	61,036	80,334	37,167	91,255	332,175
1974	5,203	45,520	54,571	61,039	32,427	73,092	271,852
1973	4,484	36,876	45,094	51,129	24,655	59,322	221,560
1972	5,256	34,079	45,258	45,714	22,945	52,014	205,266

Annual Rates of Growth - Per Cent

1972-82	+8.7	+12.9	+14.8	+15.3	+10.6	+15.4	+14.2
1977-82	+3.3	+7.8	+18.4	+11.6	+9.5	+9.8	+11.4
1972-77	+14.5	+18.4	+11.2	+19.2	+11.8	+21.0	+17.1

Notes: These figures have been grossed up for changes of threshold since 1977. Royalties are excluded.
* Hardback; bibles in paperback included in 'other'
Source: Business Monitor

1980, which was 33 per cent greater than in 1977. While there was a 10½ per cent decline in 1981, this was more than offset by a 12 per cent rise the following year, while in 1983 the rate of growth that had prevailed in the 1972-82 period was re-established with a rise in the total number of titles published of 5.7 per cent.

Publishing activity shows responsiveness to cyclical economic downturns in the reduction in the number of titles issued in 1974 and 1981. Long lead times, however, give rise to a somewhat erratic pattern, and, over the five-year spans covered in the table, there appears, paradoxically, to be an inverse relationship between the rate of growth in turnover and that of titles issued.

The Business Monitor statistics also provide a breakdown of turnover by subject matter (Table 12), illustrating some wide variations in the pattern of sales. One general feature, however, is a slowing down of growth rates in the 1977-82 period, compared to 1972-77.

The underperformance of children's books (Table 12) is consistent with population patterns in the UK, the numbers in the 0-9 age bracket having fallen by almost 2 million or 22 per cent between 1971 and 1981. Undoubtedly, however, many factors other than population trends have also influenced these results. A major underperformer has been bibles in hardback, where exports account for some three-fifths of the total. It is of some interest to note, however, that US bible exports have achieved a 14½ per cent compound growth rate over the same ten-year period (Table 66). In the more recent five-year period most of the other sectors have kept fairly close to the average growth rate for the industry at current prices.

Further Analysis of Subjects

Euromonitor Publications have calculated domestic sales for twenty-three sectors. The Euromonitor estimates are expressed in retail values (not publishers' receipts) and derive from their own estimates of publishers' domestic turnover which are some 13 per cent lower than those calculated by the Publishers Association, ie £665m against £764m for 1982.

According to the classification in Table 13, fiction represents some 48½ per cent of the total UK domestic non-institutional market; within that definition, there are three major constituents, romance, crime/thriller and the modern/classic novel. In non-fiction, the one category of comparable size to these is history. Next come biography and education.

Euromonitor also provides estimates of the total UK market (retail and institutional) expressed in prices to the final purchaser (Table 14). While the categories are less detailed than in the preceding table, their merit is that they aim to be comprehensive.

14

Table 13

Estimated Value of Retail Sales at Current Prices - 1982

(£millions)	Paperback	Hardback	TOTAL
Fiction,	200	95	295
of which			
romance	50	10	60
historical	15	10	25
crime/thriller	30	20	50
modern/classic novel	35	15	50
fantasy (sci-fi/			
horror/occult)	30	5	35
war/adventure	20	10	30
all children's	15	15	30
other fiction	5	10	15
Non-fiction,	120	195	315
of which			
history	15	35	50
biography	25	15	40
education	10	30	40
sport & leisure	15	20	35
children's	15	20	35
business/technical	10	15	25
cookery/diet	7	13	20
animals/nature	2	8	10
arts & crafts	7	8	15
gardening	2	10	12
religion	1	3	4
dictionaries	1	3	4
atlases	1	2	3
encyclopaedias	1	3	4
other	8	10	18
TOTAL	320	290	610

Note: The figures relate to final sales of the retail sector, and are after allowance for returns. Sales to the institutional sector are excluded.
Source: The Book Report, 1983, Euromonitor Publications

In Table 14, mass-market paperback corresponds broadly to the paperback fiction total of the preceding table. In terms of the total industry, fiction is estimated to account for one-quarter of turnover, non-fiction for 29 per cent and children's books for 12 per cent. The remaining third is broadly instructional in character, comprising reference, school textbooks and further education books.

Table 14

Retail Value of Total UK Market at Current Prices by Subject - 1982

(£millions)	Mass-market paperbacks	Other	TOTAL at Retail value	
Total	220	350	570	66.3
Fiction	125	90	215	25.0
Non-fiction	60	190	250	29.1
Children's	35	70	105	12.2
Reference books				
Total	105		105	12.2
Reference	40		40	4.7
Maps and guides	45		45	5.2
Bibles etc	20		20	2.3
School Textbooks				
Total school textbooks	80		80	9.3
Further Education books				
Total further education	105		105	12.2
Arts & social sciences	70			
Science, technology, medicine	35			
OVERALL TOTAL			860	100%

Source: The Book Report, 1983, Euromonitor Publications

The Bookseller statistics of titles published provide a yet more detailed view of the differing experience of various sub-ject areas, which are broken down into 46 separate categories, (Table 15). Moreover, while Tables 13 and 14 only offer a snapshot view of UK book sales as at 1982, some slight idea of trends can be gleaned from the analysis of book titles published.

Table 15

Breakdown of All Titles Published

	Average 1971-1973	Average 1981-1983	Per cent change
Aeronautics	133	227	+71
Agriculture, forestry	247	463	+87
Architecture	358	386	+ 8
Art	1,034	1,325	+28
Astronomy	83	149	+80
Bibliography, library economy	543	746	+37
Biography	1,043	1,568	+50
Chemistry, physics	896	711	-21
Children's	2,296	3,100	+35
Commerce	820	1,361	+66
Customs, costumes, folklore	123	167	+36
Domestic science	395	751	+90
Education	977	1,212	+24
Engineering	1,153	1,621	+40
Entertainment	393	648	+65
Fiction	3,863	4,964	+29
General	168	730	+335
Geography, archaeology	306	532	+74
Geology, meteorology	235	369	+57
History	1,500	1,558	+ 4
Humour	81	209	+158
Industry	461	558	+21
Language	332	676	+104
Law, public administration	972	1,550	+59
Literature	1,060	1,650	+56
Mathematics	586	887	+51
Medical science	1,459	3,092	+112
Military science	167	141	-16
Music	275	451	+64
Natural science	1,050	1,306	+24
Occultism	198	211	+ 7
Philosophy	348	549	+58
Photography	76	266	+250
Plays	275	297	+ 8
Poetry	825	780	- 5
Political science, economy	2,764	4,068	+47
Psychology	441	755	+71
Radio/TV	185	291	+57
Religion, theology	1,138	1,825	+60
School textbooks	1,853	1,921	+ 4
Science general	94	63	-33
Sociology	770	1,122	+46
Sports, outdoor games	466	554	+19
Stock breeding	170	275	+62
Trade	376	568	+51
Travel guidebooks	655	834	+27
TOTAL	33,643	47,487	+41

Source: The Bookseller

The sectors that have seen the most rapid growth of titles (65 per cent and over) are identified, as are those that have been at the bottom of the league table (where the number of titles has risen by 25 per cent or less). The average for all titles works out at growth of 41 per cent.

Table 16

Book Titles Published

Average 1971-1973 to 1981-1983 65 per cent and over		Average 1971-1973 to 1981-1983 25 per cent or less	
General	+335	Science, general	-33
Photography	+250	Chemistry, physics	-21
Humour	+158	Military science	-16
Medical science	+112	Poetry	-5
Language	+104	School textbooks	+4
Domestic science, cookery	+90	History	+4
Agriculture*	+87	Occultism	+7
Astronomy	+80	Plays	+8
Geography/archaeology	+74	Architecture	+8
Psychology	+71	Sports, outdoor games	+19
Aeronautics	+71	Industry	+21
Commerce	+66	Natural Science	+24
Entertainment	+65	Education	+24

* Including forestry, gardening

It must be admitted that 'titles published' in a particular sector can give a distorted impression where the absolute figures are small: the discovery of humour as number three in the plus column and military science as number three in the minus column could, if taken at face value, encourage undue optimism on the perfectibility of human nature. Sluggish enrolment figures are no doubt reflected in the decline in chemistry and physics and general science, as well as in subnormal growth of school textbooks. The shift of emphasis away from the humanities is also featured, though 'literature' itself, having risen strongly from 1,151 titles in 1981 to 2,187 titles in 1983 is safe with above average expansion of 56 per cent. Within the growth column, the strength of subjects of a practical character emerges quite clearly.

Foreign Trade

The deceleration in export sales over the last ten years, which is a marked feature of the Publishers Association export

18

Table 17

Exports of Printed Books

(£thousands)	1955	1965	1972	1977	1979
Country of destination					
Australia	1,178	4,401	10,208	26,678	31,531
New Zealand	469	1,063	1,837	5,643	7,725
Canada	588	1,790	5,170	10,800	9,331
Nigeria	-	-	2,958	24,334	16,247
Irish Republic	264	567	2,666	6,259	10,209
South Africa	347	1,510	3,232	5,415	8,504
EEC (6)	499	1,905	11,289	22,126	28,144
USA	1,601	5,907	18,525	36,585	42,186
All other	2,723*	8,222*	13,403	40,117	55,416
TOTAL	7,669	25,365	69,288	177,957	209,293

(£thousands)	1980	1981	1982	Eleven months 1982	Eleven months 1983
Australia	26,585	31,015	37,621	35,088	40,341
New Zealand	6,758	8,061	8,159	7,604	9,663
Canada	8,782	12,262	10,781	9,552	12,965
Nigeria	30,411	37,987	20,972	19,292	9,402
Irish Republic	11,872	10,826	13,876	12,828	14,938
South Africa	13,370	17,879	20,693	18,719	18,666
EEC (6)	33,957	32,952	36,711	33,500	39,537
USA	44,077	44,030	50,427	45,416	53,994
All other	61,454	74,233	88,645	80,896	92,165
TOTAL	237,266	269,245	287,885	262,895	291,671

Note: These figures include booklets, brochures, pamphlets and leaflets. They exclude freight costs. * Includes Nigeria
Source: Overseas Trade Statistics

statistics presented in Table 11, is revealed in greater detail in the Overseas Trade Statistics. Differences of definition and coverage are behind the differences in the absolute figures. In both cases, the tables relate to non-inflation-adjusted values.

The phenomenon of Nigeria (Table 17) dominates the last ten years: in 1972 UK exports to Nigeria were £2.96m, 4¼ per cent of total book exports and at their peak in 1981 they amounted to £37.99m - a thirteenfold increase in nine years - when they represented a vulnerable 14 per cent of the total. It should, incidentally, be noted in this connection that the trade statistics are not adjusted for 'non-performing' receivables in the hands of the British exporters, to employ the expression to which bankers have become used. The table also highlights the subsequent collapse, with exports falling by 45 per cent in 1982 from their peak levels and halving again in the first eleven months of 1983.

The main export market that has gone against the trend of slowing sales is South Africa, where sales, after lagging markedly in the first five years, 1972-77, expanded at a rate of 30.7 per cent in the subsequent five years and in 1982 represented 7.2 per cent of UK book exports against 3.0 per cent in 1977. A rapidly expanding economy and none of the shrinkage that occurs when indigenous publishing replaces imported books are behind this pattern.

The Irish Republic has also been a market where UK export growth has been well sustained, and the same holds true of the residual 'all other' classification. The EEC (the original six) has proved to be a less volatile market than many.

Table 18

Percentage Changes in UK Book Exports

(per cent)	1972-1982 TOTAL	1972-1977 Annual Rates	1977-1982 Annual Rates	1972-1982 Annual Rates
TOTAL	+315	+21.0	+10.1	+15.3
Australia	+269	+21.2	+ 7.1	+13.9
New Zealand	+344	+25.3	+ 7.6	+16.1
Canada	+108	+15.9	-	+ 7.6
Nigeria	+608	+52.3	- 2.9	+21.6
Irish Republic	+420	+18.6	+17.3	+17.9
South Africa	+540	+10.9	+30.7	+20.4
EEC (6)	+225	+14.4	+10.6	+12.5
USA	+172	+14.6	+ 6.6	+10.5
All other	+561	+24.5	+17.2	+20.8

20

Below-average growth has been a feature of sales to Canada and the USA and, in the more recent period, to Australia and New Zealand.

The latest available figures which cover the first eleven months of 1983 show a rise of 10.9 per cent over the same period a year earlier. This is at a time when the general level of UK inflation is hovering around 5 per cent and suggests a degree of real growth. If Nigeria is taken out of the figures, the rise comes to a very respectable 15.9 per cent, with all of the other countries and areas identified in the table contributing, barring South Africa which has been going through a recession that has been out of phase with that of many other countries.

The sensitivity of exports to currency changes is a subject that invites prolonged debate. Table 19 provides ammunition to both sides. Where the relationship is least clear is in the broad aggregates - the index of effective exchange rates in relation to overall exports. This is perhaps not altogether surprising given the influence on total exports of swings in shipments to Nigeria, for example, where price is swamped by other considerations.

Table 19

Currency Changes and Book Exports

	1977	1978	1979	1980	1981	1982	1983
(Average Exchange Rates)							
Index (a)	81.3	81.5	87.3	96.2	93.3	89.5	82.3
US $	1.78	1.93	2.16	2.33	1.97	1.71	1.48
C. $	1.90	2.24	2.53	2.74	2.36	2.13	1.83
A. $	1.59	1.68	1.94	2.02	1.72	1.71	1.68
SA.R	1.57	1.69	1.81	1.78	1.76	1.89	1.68
(Book exports)							
£m (b)	178.0	206.5	209.3	237.3	269.2	287.9	318.2+

+ Eleven months annualized.
Sources: (a) Index of effective exchange rates published by the Bank of England (b) Overseas Trade Statistics

The best 'fit' is achieved in the case of the USA, where UK exports (with a one-year time-lag) have shown themselves to be highly responsive to changes in the value of sterling against the dollar (Table 20).

Table 20

Relationship of UK Exports to the USA/changes in the £:$ rate

(per cent)	1978	1979	1980	1981	1982	1983*
UK exports	+17.4	-1.8	+4.5	-0.1	+14.5	+18.9
£:$ rate	+8.4	+11.9	+7.9	-15.5	-13.3	-13.5

* Eleven months

Turning to imports, while there has been a modest slowing down in the rates of growth over the two five-year periods 1972-77 and 1977-82, this has been insignificant compared to the deceleration in exports.

Table 21

Imports of Printed Books

(£thousands) Country of origin	1955	1965	1972	1977	1979
EEC (6)	870	2,643	7,229	17,967	30,711
USA	975	4,819	10,716	26,509	37,696
All other	507	2,559	9,488	24,166	34,732
TOTAL	2,352	10,021	27,433	68,642	103,139

(£thousands)	1980	1981	1982	Eleven months 1982	Eleven months 1983
EEC (6)	31,025+	27,445	37,162	32,174	39,992
USA	49,620	56,116	56,756	64,311	72,024
All other	43,436	62,007	68,462	61,998	65,716
TOTAL	124,081	145,568	162,380	158,483	177,732

Note: These figures include booklets, brochures, pamphlets and leaflets. They exclude children's picture books.
+ Partly estimated
Source: Overseas Trade Statistics

In the five-year period, 1972-77, the three separate areas identified in the table expanded at approximately the same speed. The period 1977-82, however, witnessed a significant divergence, with imports from the residual category rising at an above-average rate. This reflects to a significant extent shipments back to the UK of British publishers' books manufactured overseas, notably in the Far East, under the stimulus of a rising exchange rate. Imports from Hong Kong and Singapore, for example, came to £24.6m in 1981, equivalent to 16.9 per cent of all book imports; in 1972 the figure had been £1.35m and the proportion 4.9 per cent.

Table 22

Percentage Changes in UK Book Imports

(per cent)	1972-1982 TOTAL	1972-1977 Annual Rates	1977-1982 Annual Rates	1972-1982 Annual Rates
TOTAL	+492	+20.1	+18.8	+19.5
EEC (6)	+414	+20.0	+15.6	+17.8
USA	+430	+19.9	+16.4	+18.1
All other	+622	+20.6	+23.2	+21.8

The deceleration in the rate of expansion of imports since 1980 is broadly consistent with the change in the value of the pound which might have been expected to discourage overseas manufacture by UK publishers and to inhibit, on price grounds, retail sales of imported books. Indeed, in 1980 imports rose 20 per cent, in 1981 17 per cent and in 1982 12 per cent. What is harder to explain is the maintenance in the first eleven months of 1983 of a rapid rate of increase in book imports, which advanced 12 per cent, with imports from the EEC being particularly strong. Also, this is in the face of anecdotal evidence of many publishers repatriating to the UK manufacturing that they previously placed abroad.

Taking the full period 1955-82, imports have grown considerably more rapidly than exports. But since, in absolute terms, exports exceed imports by a sizeable margin, the positive trade balance on books has continued to expand, having been £5.3m in 1955, £41.9m in 1972 and £125.5m in 1982. In 1983, however, the eleven month figures would suggest a positive balance for the year that is slightly down on 1982 at £124m.

Inflation Adjusted Publishers' Sales

The analysis so far has concentrated on turnover unadjusted for inflation. Accounting for inflation is one of the more problematical exercises when considering the UK publishing industry statistics. Table 23 gives the results of deflating publishers' turnover when taking differing measures of inflation. The turnover series chosen are:
(a) the Business Monitor turnover figures grossed up for non-reporting, (Table 11);
(b) the Business Monitor figures, not grossed up but adjusted for alterations to the basis on which the figures are collected, notably in respect of thresholds of reporting, (Table 12).
The deflators require some comment: The Book Price Index is based on a monthly recording of a representative sample of books sold at a representative sample of retail outlets distributed throughout the country. By definition, it ignores sales

Table 23

Publishing Turnover Adjusted for Inflation

	Total PA	Turnover Bus.Mon*	Adjusted by Book Price Index		Adjusted by All Items RPI		Adjusted by Bookseller Index	
	£m	£m	(A)	(B)	(A)	(B)	(A)	(B)
1982	1,100	777	88.8	88.5	102.2	102.6	107.3	106.4
1981	1,077	764	98.0	97.4	108.6	107.9	119.7	119.3
1980	976	693	104.4	104.1	110.2	107.3	120.3	119.7
1979	844	598	106.0	104.4	112.3	109.9	119.8	119.4
1978	751	535	104.4	103.3	113.4	110.7	114.4	114.5
1977	653	452	104.6	101.3	106.8	103.5	110.9	107.9
1976	563	393	109.0	107.3	106.7	103.4	106.9	104.8
1975	469	332	106.2	105.2	103.6	103.6	112.3	111.7
1974	384	272	108.7	108.6	105.3	104.6	117.3	116.7
1973	314	222	104.4	103.6	99.9	99.3	108.4	107.6
1972	288	205	100.0	100.0	100.0	100.0	100.0	100.0

* Excludes royalties
(A) Calculated on the total grossed up turnover
(B) Calculated on the Business Monitor turnover as adjusted by the Publishers Association for changes in reporting thresholds
Sources: Derived from: Quarterly Statistics, September 1983; The Publishers Association; The Bookseller, August 20, 1983

to the academic and institutional markets. While recognizing this to be a substantial defect, the Publishers Association on balance prefers the BPI to the alternatives. The Retail Price Index encompasses the Book Price Index and is a comprehensive index covering all aspects of consumer expenditure. The Bookseller index is the average of all titles published unweighted for length of run; the figures are presented in Table 11.

The first point to make is that, however adjusted for price changes, publishing turnover showed at best only modest growth in the period 1972-80 and subsequently fell off sharply as the recession made itself felt. Secondly, if the grossed up totals are chosen, the industry consistently performed less badly than if the Business Monitor figures are chosen. My own preference for the former as an overall indicator of the true state of affairs is reinforced by the knowledge that the returns from the Publishers Association's own Collection Scheme, which dates from 1977, give results that are better than those indicated by the Business Monitor statistics. More generally, the apparently endless succession of changes in the composition and presentation of the government figures - we are promised further alterations for 1983 - and the frequent delays in their publication do not inspire confidence.

Table 24

Breakdown of Publishers' Turnover - Index of Volume

Year	Bibles*	School textbks	Tech & scient	Fiction Lit Classics	Children's	Other	TOTAL
1982	54.1	79.0	92.5	97.2	64.4	93.6	88.5
1981	61.2	96.1	95.9	104.5	70.7	104.4	97.4
1980	69.1	102.1	91.7	109.4	76.6	121.8	104.1
1979	65.6	102.5	79.4	108.2	86.3	129.5	104.4
1978	80.6	104.5	76.6	114.6	81.1	123.7	103.3
1977	90.5	107.0	78.2	110.6	80.4	117.3	101.3
1976	103.0	110.4	84.8	117.2	93.8	120.6	107.3
1975	87.3	105.5	87.7	114.2	105.3	111.6	105.2
1974	81.2	109.5	98.9	109.5	115.9	112.1	108.6
1973	81.9	103.9	95.7	107.4	103.2	107.0	103.6
1972	100.0	100.0	100.0	100.0	100.0	100.0	100.0

* Hardback bibles; also included in 'other' together with paperback bibles. Note: Adjusted by The Book Price Index
Source: Business Monitor

Sadly, however, when it comes to the analysis of inflation-adjusted turnover, it is hard to avoid using the Business Monitor. Table 24 provides some indication of the relative performance of six broad sectors.

Even allowing for the fact that the price deflator used (the Government Book Price Index) is harsher than other inflation measures, the evidence of contraction - massive in some instances - is undoubtedly powerful. The point must naturally be made, however, that the choice of 1982 as the year marking the end of the period studied distorts the picture in as much as 1982 saw the trough of the worst post-war depression experienced by this country. Also, it should be noted that domestic sales held up very much better than exports, a fact that is implicit in the earlier discussion of international trade statistics. And if one goes back to Table 10 the picture of UK consumer expenditure on books as a proportion of total outlays being well maintained is undoubtedly comforting. In Table 25 the inflation-adjusted home and export performance broken down by sector is presented.

The most significant areas of export weakness relative to home sales have been bibles, children's books, technical and scientific textbooks and fiction. As already indicated at various stages of the present discussion, the massive relative underperformance of exports owes something to the non-recording of certain exports since 1980, to the delayed impact of a pound which made its high in the first quarter of 1981 and to the development of indigenous publishing at the expense of exports.

Table 25

Index of Inflation Adjusted Turnover by Selected Sectors 1972-1982+

	Home	Export	Total
School textbooks	76.0	83.2	79.0
Technical & scientific	111.2	68.9	92.5
Fiction, literature & classics	110.8	69.9	97.2
Children's	66.1	58.6	64.4
Bibles*	96.6	37.6	54.1
Other	96.9	85.8	93.6
TOTAL	95.6	75.1	88.5

+ Adjusted by the Book Price Index, 1972 = 100
* Hardback bibles included in 'other' as in Table 24
Source: Business Monitor

5. UK Institutional Market

The Educational Sector

So as to place in context the expenditure figures on books in education, total government spending in education and science is shown in Table 26. The table covers the period 1977-78 to 1982-83 (the government's estimated out-turn in the latter year) and includes the government's projections for 1983-84. The unadjusted totals show growth from £7,039m in 1977-78 to £12,628m estimated in 1982-83, an annual rate of 12.4 per cent. Expressed in figures of constant purchasing power, however, there has been a slight erosion from a 1977-78 total of £11,922m to £11,747m estimated for 1982-83, a rate of decline of 0.3 per cent. The contraction in the school population from 8.67m to 7.72m has been that much more rapid at 2.3 per cent per annum, while the numbers of teachers fell by 1.2 per cent per annum.

Table 26

Government Expenditure - Education & Science - School Population

	1977-78	1979-80	1981-82	1982-83	1983-84*
Education & Science (£millions)					
Total public expenditure (central government and local authority)	7,039	8,946	11,828	12,628	12,560
(Total in 1981-82 £)	(11,922)	(11,709)	(11,828)	(11,747)	(11,127)
Total current expenditure	6,528	8,361	11,231	12,076	12,033
of which, pay	4,275	5,315	7,313	7,778	7,640
subsidies & grants	1,361	1,777	2,421	2,544	2,657
transport, milk, meals	463	557	571	605	475
other	429	712	926	1,149	1,261
School Population - England					
School population (thousands)	8,666	8,397	7,973	7,722	7,505
Teachers (thousands)	436	438	420	411	up to 400

* Government projection
Source: The Government's Expenditure Plans 1983-84 to 1985-86, February 1983, HMSO

Expenditure on books is included under the residual 'other' category, which showed a rise over the five-year period to 1982-83 of 21.7 per cent per annum. If these figures are then related to the spending statistics on books presented in Table 27, the relative sluggishness of educational book purchases becomes apparent: over the whole period 1975 to 1981, spending

Table 27

Educational Expenditure on Books

(£millions)	1975	1976	1977	1978	1979	1980	1981
England & Wales							
Primary schools	14.8	16.8	18.1	19.9	21.2	23.2	24.6
Secondary schools	19.5	23.3	25.9	28.8	31.4	32.4	34.1
Nursery and special schools	0.5	0.6	0.9	0.9	1.0	1.0	1.0
Sub-total	34.8	40.7	44.9	49.6	53.6	56.6	59.7
Polytechnics	4.2	5.9	6.5	6.9	7.0	6.8	9.1
Other further education	6.0	7.0	7.9	8.3	9.0	9.6	9.6
TOTAL	45.0	53.6	59.3	64.8	69.6	73.0	78.4
Scotland & N.I.	6.0	7.0	8.0	8.0	10.0	12.0	13.0
University libraries - UK	6.0	6.9	8.1	9.2	9.5	10.6	10.6
TOTAL, UK	57.1	67.6	75.5	82.0	89.1	95.6	102.0

Note: The table excludes expenditures by private organizations. Discrepancies are due to rounding.
Sources: The Book Report, 1983, Euromonitor Publications; The Supply of Books to Schools and Colleges, The Booksellers Association, 1981; The Publishers Association, Educational Publishers Council

on books in England and Wales in primary and secondary schools grew at a rate of 9.4 per cent, while over the four years 1977 to 1981 (the closest match with the period covered in Table 26) the rate of increase was 7.4 per cent, both well below the rates of growth in overall Government outlays.

In higher education, the student numbers represented in Table 28 include university undergraduates in Great Britain, advanced course students other than at university in England and home students (full time and sandwich). Non-advanced further education relates to England and includes home students.

Table 28

Higher and Further Education Student Numbers

(thousands)	1980-81	1981-82	1982-83	1983-84
Higher education	394	415	429	NA
Non-advanced further education	482	507	534	548

Source: The Government's Expenditure Plans 1983-84 to 1985-86, February 1983, HMSO

While the numbers have been advancing, the downward pressures on government funding have been significant. By 1984/85, as pointed out in the review of the Government's Expenditure Plans, the present phase of contraction for higher education should have come to an end; by then there will have been a loss of one out of every six academic members of staff.

Looking ahead, demographics will continue to have on balance a depressing influence throughout the 1980s in the school sector. The school population figures in Table 29 differ from those shown in Table 26 through inclusion of direct grant and independent schools.

The pattern in Table 29 is, not surprisingly, broadly the same as that provided in the UK population projections (Table 3), with the primary population suffering the greatest contraction in the 1981-86 period, to be followed by the secondary school population between 1986 and 1991. It is remarkable that secondary school enrolment in England is due to drop by over 1 million between 1981 and 1991, a fall of more than 25 per cent. The encouraging feature of the table is the general, albeit modest, upturn at all levels projected for the period 1991-96.

Table 29

Estimated School Population - England

(thousands)	1971	1976	1981	1986	1991	1996
TOTAL	8,325	9,181	8,630	7,631	7,351	7,870
Under five	284	397	361	329	357	366
Primary	4,755	4,726	4,087	3,563	3,886	4,124
Secondary	3,286	4,059	4,182	3,739	3,108	3,380

Source: Department of Education and Science

In terms of expenditure on books, the near-term outlook cannot be characterized as in any way buoyant. Much, however, must depend on the general economic situation and on the way in which local authorities manage their affairs in an environment which, initially at least, will be comparatively free of inflationary pressures. The point is made in respect of 1983-84 in the government's report on its expenditure plans: on assumptions that include a 4 per cent pay increase together with a reduction of 2½ per cent in the number of teachers, the achievement of the target for March 1984 for 630,000 surplus school places to be taken out of use, and a general containment of costs 'it should be possible for the majority of local authorities to improve their provision per pupil for new books and equipment compared with 1980-81 and to restore in 1983-84 and then maintain up to 1985-86 the amount of repairs and maintainance'.

Public Libraries

At 31 March 1982 the total number of central and branch libraries came to 4,765, of which 2,557 fell into the category of those open for 30-60 hours per week, 1,381 10-30 hours, and 827 less than 10 hours. In addition, there were 691 mobile libraries and 11,346 small libraries in hospitals etc. At that date the total number of books held by the public libraries amounted to 137m of which 16.5m were reference books and the balance lending books. Book borrowings in the year came to 578.4m.

Expenditure on books by public libraries amounted in 1981 to £52.6m. In the same year, the total of all spending on educational books came to an estimated £98.6m for an overall figure for institutional outlays of £151.2m. The estimate for 1982 was £155m. These figures exclude expenditures by private organizations, shown under 'miscellaneous' in Table 31.

Table 30

Institutional Expenditure on Books in the UK

	1975	1976	1977	1978	1979	1980	1981	1982*
(£millions)								
Public libraries	29.7	32.8	37.1	44.0	47.1	48.1	52.6	56
Educational	57.1	67.6	75.5	82.0	89.1	95.6	98.6+	99
Total institutional*	86.8	100.4	112.6	126.0	136.2	143.7	151.2	155
Public libraries as % of total	34	33	33	35	35	33	35	36

* Estimate. + Shown as £102m in Table 27 on different estimates
Source: The Book Report, 1983, Euromonitor Publications, CIPFA

In the period 1975-81, public libraries have clearly maintained their relative position in institutional book purchases at a little over one third. This has entailed an annual rate of growth in expenditure of 10.0 per cent. But, when set against a rate of increase of 14.3 per cent in gross domestic product, library and educational outlays on books have been slipping within the overall economy. Furthermore, this compares to a rate of inflation in the six years of 13.9 per cent.

Books as a proportion of total public library expenditure have fallen from 24 per cent in 1966-67 to 17 per cent in 1979-80, and to an estimated 15 per cent in 1982-83. In the face of this kind of secular trend, it is hard to generate any sustained optimism. It remains true, however, that an economic upturn involving an expansion of government revenues should eventually provide an opportunity for increased spending. On these grounds, in the medium term, an improvement in book purchases can be anticipated with a fair degree of confidence. In the short term, the vagaries of local authorities spending up to their budgets can make for relatively buoyant conditions in the midst of a depressed market. It is also the case, as discussed later, that the silver lining to the public libraries' financial cloud is to be found in their rapidly spreading acceptance of paperbacks.

6. UK Distribution

An attempt is made in Table 31 to provide an approximate break-down of UK book sales at retail prices. The information has been derived from three sources, the Price Commission report which appeared in 1978 and covered the period up to 1976, the Cranfield Report which appeared in 1982 and covered the period up to 1980, and the Euromonitor Book Report of 1983 which relates to 1982. Once again, the difficulties of definition and the

Table 31

UK Market for Books - Estimated

	Price Commission 1976		Cranfield Report 1980		Euromonitor Book Report 1982	
	(£m)	(%)	(£m)	(%)	(£m)	(%)
TOTAL sales at retail value	300	100	708	100	860	100
Total institutional	99	33	186	26	250	29
Education authorities	34	11	85	12	99	12
Public libraries	33	11	48	7	56	6
Miscellaneous*	32	11	53	7	95	11
Total consumer	201	67	522	74	610	71
Book clubs	18	6	50	7	50	6
Other mail order	6	2	30	4	30	3
W H Smith	41	14	104	15	120	14
Menzies	11	4			30	3
Variety, department stores	12	4			45	5
Other bookshops			338	48	210	25
CTNs	113	37			60	7
Other outlets					65	8

* Purchases by companies, administrative authorities, other private organizations
Sources: Cranfield School of Management Report on UK Book Publishing and Distribution, 1982; Prices, Costs and Margins in the Publishing, Printing and Binding and Distribution of Books, Price Commission, June 1978; The Book Report, 1983, Euromonitor; Quarterly Statistical Bulletin, March 1981, The Publishers Association

shortcomings of much of the statistical material that is available mean that the table must be used with caution.

As is emphasized in the Cranfield Report, the extent of the contacts that the publisher has direct with the retailer is significant and stems in part from the comparative weakness of the wholesale channels:
(a) An estimated 54 per cent of the market value of books goes direct to retail outlets;
(b) of that 54 per cent, 10 per cent is then sold on to libraries and schools by those retailers who combine a library supply/educational supply role with retailing;
(c) 9 per cent of publishers' sales goes direct to firms that are exclusively library suppliers and educational contractors;
(d) 23 per cent goes to wholesalers;
(e) book clubs and direct mail account for the remaining 14 per cent.

Distribution to Education Authorities

The supply of books to schools and colleges is undertaken in three ways:
(a) through direct purchase by local authorities from publishers;
(b) through purchase by local authorities from specialist contractors, themselves supplied by publishers; and
(c) through purchase by local authorities from bookshops.

Table 32

UK Pattern of Supply of Educational Books to Local Authorities 1980

	(£m)	(%)
Direct purchase	7.5	11
Specialist contractors	17.0	25
Bookshops	43.5	64
TOTAL	68.0	100

Source: The Supply of Books to Schools and Colleges, Committee of Enquiry, Lady David, 1981

The total for 1980 of £68m (Table 32) includes an estimated £7m spent by local education authorities on books provided for colleges and polytechnics. Adjusting for this brings the total spent for schools down to £61m. At the same time, the 1979 total in Table 27 of £53.6m needs to be increased by over £6m to include expenditure for schools in Scotland and Northern Ireland, thereby going a long way towards bridging the gap between the two sets of statistics. Reconciliation with the much larger total of £85m in Table 31 relies principally on the fact that the Cranfield statistics include outlays by education authorities on university libraries and further education establishments. As mentioned in the David report, there are 121 Local Education Authorities, some 35,000 schools and approximately 400 publishers (out of a round total of 3,000) that are regularly used by the LEAs.

Direct purchase from publishers is undertaken by several organizations (The Greater London Council, the County Councils of Leicestershire, Kent and of Warwickshire, Manchester, Newcastle upon Tyne, and a consortium of local authorities in Yorkshire, known as the Yorkshire Purchasing Organisation). They fulfil the role of educational contractors, but under local authority management. However, by no means all of the book purchases of local authorities that have access to the direct purchase system are made through the local authority organizations; it has been calculated that 100 per cent purchases would have accounted for 30 per cent of the total school market against 11 per cent (see Table 32) in practice. At the time of the reorganization of local government, some of the areas that were added to those local authorities with direct purchase organizations retained their use of other sources of supply. The report also commented that new direct purchase organizations were unlikely to be established without a considerable initial capital outlay.

Since the preparation of the Lady David report the role of direct purchasing organizations has been the subject of considerable speculation, much of it centering on expansion plans of the Yorkshire Purchasing Organisation. The YPO took the decision in principle in 1983 to expand into the supply of children's books to public libraries. It would expect to receive trade terms from the publishers from whom it bought direct and it would be in a position to pass some of that benefit on to the public libraries it would be supplying (without infringing the Net Book Agreement). Were this to occur and were the YPO's initiative to be followed by other direct purchasing organizations, this would no doubt pose a serious threat to many booksellers.

There are twelve specialist educational contractors, a number of whom supply, in addition to books, other items used by schools. Their share of the market is 25 per cent.

Bookshops, as indicated in Table 32, account for the great bulk of the market with a 64 per cent share. By definition,

34

bookshops combine retailing with their role as specialist contractors. In 1980, 220 held book supply contracts with local authorities in the UK; in addition, a further 400 booksellers were involved in the school book market - supplying authorities but without there being a contractual arrangement and supplying individual schools, often in respect of library and school prize purchases. The importance of non-retail business to certain bookshops is illustrated in the results of a survey undertaken in 1972 by the Booksellers Association: those stockholding bookshops that traded with educational establishments (including public libraries) were shown to have derived 49 per cent of their turnover from such business.

In another analysis, it was shown that library books bought by schools accounted in 1979-80 for 28 per cent of all educational book purchases. These being net books, margins are that much higher than on the non-library business. In more recent times, with local authorities in a financial squeeze, economy measures have frequently involved cutting down on the library purchases (high margin business for the bookseller) in order better to maintain textbook purchases (on which margins are typically low). This development has undoubtedly had an important bearing on the poor financial results in recent years of bookselling as a whole.

The overall conclusion of the report is that it is neither desirable (nor particularly likely) that significant changes should take place in the methods by which books are distributed to UK educational authorities.

Distribution to Public Libraries

The supply of books to public libraries is primarily through library suppliers, some of whom are specialists that often double as educational contractors and some booksellers with a library supply activity. The specialists number up to twenty. On average, library supply is more important to booksellers than is educational supply.

The year 1982 witnessed some important developments among specialist library suppliers, with John Menzies acquiring, in May 1982, Combridge Jackson in the UK and James Bennett in Australia through its £6.3m purchase of Lonsdale Universal, and acquiring, in July 1982 for £3.85m, Collier Macmillan Distributors Services (previously Woolstons & Blunt). Up to that point John Menzies' involvement in library supply had been confined to the library business of a number of its retail shops. As a result of these purchases Menzies secured some 23 per cent of the UK market, putting it well ahead of Blackwell's with about 15 per cent. In 1983, the company purchased John Coutts Library Services based in Niagara, Canada and with a subsidiary at Lewiston, New York. These moves make Menzies the largest library supplier in Canada, Australia and the UK and give it a useful presence in the USA.

Table 33

Share of Charter Group Sales to Libraries and Schools

Year to March 31 (per cent)	1976-77	1977-78	1978-79	1979-80	1980-81	1981-82
Library supply	9.3	8.0	9.4	8.9	8.2	7.1
Educational supply	6.7	5.4	5.5	3.7	4.2	3.5

Source: Charter Group Economic Surveys, published in The Bookseller, January 1983

Menzies entry into the library supply market was the result of a number of considerations. Firstly, the nature of the business of library supply which is characterized by a multiplicity of small orders, brings it closer to retailing than to educational supply, and therefore to an activity with which Menzies was already familiar. Secondly, a large group such as Menzies has developed considerable expertise in modern computer systems used in retailing, and management saw library supply as a promising further area in which to apply these skills. And thirdly, following the company's success in acquiring a dominant stake in the business in the course of a few months, by means of two acquisitions, the scope for achieving economies of scale could well prove significant.

Aside from such domestic considerations, Menzies were also eager to develop the international character of library supply. Combridge Jackson's own business involves providing a book-selling service to public libraries primarily in Continental Europe and the Middle East as well as the UK, while James Bennett are well established as library book suppliers throughout Australasia and the Far East. James Bennett also has a presence in North America, where Menzies' position has been greatly strengthened by the purchase of John Coutts. The company's goal is to be able to give libraries throughout the countries in which it is established a service covering world-wide bibliographic data and the supply of a wide range of English language publications together with a comprehensive serials service. This is also seen as meeting the particular requirements of international libraries. To this end, books will be stocked in Australia, Canada and the USA, as well as the UK, and Menzies will have their own specialized sales forces in those countries. The present scale of operations is indicated by a turnover which is estimated to be in excess of £25m.

In general, Menzies sees the supply of books to libraries as having greater prospects of growth outside the UK than within.

In terms of profits, however, the scope in the UK looks attractive, as well as overseas.

Book Clubs

Book clubs in Table 31 are shown as accounting for between 6 per cent and 7 per cent of the total UK book sales at retail value. This compares with an estimated 3 per cent in 1974 and 1½ per cent in 1953.

The post-war period has been marked by some important modifications to the Publishers Association regulations governing the operation of book clubs in the UK and this has led to changes in the nature of the business and in the participants.

The immediate post-war period saw substantial growth in membership of book clubs. These sold reprints of existing titles - after a year (now nine months) had elapsed since original publication - at a discount below the original publication price which was determined by the book club and might be of the order of 60 per cent to 70 per cent. Membership in such clubs rose at one stage to an estimated one million (Table 34). In the 1960s, however, the earlier impetus weakened, in part as a result of the development of paperbacks which satisfied much the same desire for economy. The Companion Book Club which had more than 400,000 members, saw that figure decline below 100,000 and the Reprint Society, which had had some 250,000 members suffered an eclipse that eventually saw membership down to less than 50,000. The relaxation in 1963 of certain restrictions, notably the concession that enabled book clubs to offer premium books to new members, helped to halt the slide in membership, not to reverse it.

The most important regulatory change, however, occurred in February, 1968, when the Publishers Association authorized the simultaneous publication of book club editions of new books, priced at discounts of up to 25 per cent for non-fiction, 35 per cent for fiction.

This change brought UK practice closer into line with that of other countries, notably the USA. In that connection, it was important for the subsequent rapid growth of book clubs in the UK that Book Club Associates should have been formed in 1966, being a 50/50 partnership between W. H. Smith and Doubleday. The latter remains one of the most experienced book club publishers in the USA where its flagship is the Book of the Month Club. BCA itself took over W. H. Smith's embryonic Direct Book Service and also acquired control of the Reprint Society. Following the decision on simultaneous book club editions, BCA launched the Literary Guild in the autumn of 1968 as its first simultaneous book club, while continuing to promote its reprint clubs, the largest being World Books.

The next few years witnessed a rash of new clubs in the UK; this included the development of special interest clubs as well

37

as those of more general appeal. Certain changes of ownership also occurred, notably the acquisition by BCA in 1977 of Purnell's book clubs (History Book Club, Military History Book Club, Cookery Book Club). And on the regulatory front, in 1974 the Publishers Association gave simultaneous book clubs the freedom to offer unlimited discounts subject to the approval of the licensing hardback publisher.

The rapid expansion of book clubs, which is highlighted in the membership estimates in Table 34 was fuelled, in part, by new entrants. What was widely regarded as being of considerable potential importance was the entry in 1977 into the UK market of Bertelsmann, the major publishing group having a considerable international presence in book clubs. Bertelsmann's initial move was the launch of Leisure Circle, a general interest book club, having the exceptional characteristic for UK book clubs of being marketed by door to door salesmen (now 300) as well as through advertising and by direct mail. And in 1979, as further evidence of the growth expectations many shared in book clubs at the time, the Nationwide Book Club was formed, being jointly owned by William Collins, William Heinemann and Bonnier.

Table 34

Book Clubs in the UK - Estimated Membership

(thousands)	Late 1950s	1974	1981
BCA (25 clubs*)	NA	500	1,250
Leisure Circle	NA	NA	150
Nationwide	NA	NA	170
Readers Union (10 clubs*)	40	60	150
Foyles (10 clubs*))		50	30
Folio Society)	310	30	35
Purnell)		90	
Odhams/Companion	400+	90	50
Reprint Society	250	NA	NA
TOTAL	1,000+	820	1,835

*1981. Sources: The Book Report, 1981, Euromonitor; Retail Business, August 1974, Economist Intelligence Unit; 'Book Clubs on the March Again', Laurence Cotterell, The Bookseller, October 16, 1976.

Some indication of this pattern of book club growth, contraction and renewed growth in the post-war period is given in Table 34.

More so than ever, the figures in Table 34 must be regarded as estimates. In the light of Leisure Circle's stated ambition to obtain one million members, and the 'development phase' in which it finds itself, the 150,000 membership estimate must be treated with particular caution; one other source gave membership at the end of 1981 as 300,000.

In more recent experience, it is undeniable that book clubs suffered severely from the recession and that their relatively down-market profile of membership made them particularly vulnerable. The sale of Nationwide to David & Charles's Readers Union in March 1982, for a nominal sum, was striking evidence of a change of heart on the part of the three major publishers that had backed Nationwide and had had to absorb cumulative losses since the original launch amounting to an estimated £5m. It is also common knowledge that the market leader, Book Club Associates, has experienced difficult trading conditions in the last two years.

In considering the post-war development of book clubs in the UK, one cannot help but be struck by the impact of regulatory changes, which have led to a regime that appears extremely liberal. It is hard to see any further massive boosts to activity coming from fresh alterations to the rules. In fact the latest change in the rules governing book clubs is restrictive as far as the largest clubs are concerned, rather than the reverse. In September 1983, the Director-General of the Office of Fair Trading agreed to drop an investigation into book clubs which had been started three years before, following an undertaking by the book clubs that they would 'voluntarily limit the extent to which they would obtain exclusive book club rights to any title'. The time limit was set at three years, down from five years previously.

While the UK is undoubtedly 'under book-clubbed' by many countries' standards, sound reasons can be presented for this, notably our more highly developed public library system. It seems also possible that the 'value for money' appeal of book clubs will remain under steady challenge from paperbacks and hardback bargain books. This is not to deny, however, the convenience factor and the contribution they make to potential readers who are bemused by the range of choice in bookshops and on bookstalls. And from the point of view of publishers, the opportunity book club orders provide for printing economically should not be lost sight of. Overall, however, the impression now given is of a relatively mature industry whose outlook is tied to general economic trends.

Retail Outlets

Estimates of retail sales by outlet were published by the Publishers Association in the Quarterly Statistical Bulletin of March 1981, broken down into hardback and paperback. In comparing the percentages with those in earlier tables, notably Table 31, it should be remembered that Table 35 relates to actual numbers of volumes. In this connection Euromonitor Publications has estimated that volume sales in the UK in 1982 amounted to 320m, of which 210m were paperback and 110m hardback. Out of this total, retail sales are estimated to have accounted for 225m (180m paperback, 45m hardback) with a sales value of £610m, and institutional sales for 95m (30m paperback and 65m hardback) with a sales value of £250m.

Table 35

Volume Breakdown of Retail Sales by Outlet - 1978

(per cent)	Hardback	Paperback	Total
W. H. Smith/J. Menzies	21	44	37
Independent bookshops	64	17	32
Variety, department stores	9	8	9
CTNs	4	18	14
Other outlets	2	13	9
TOTAL	100	100	100

Note: Discrepancies are due to rounding
Source: Quarterly Statistical Bulletin, March 1981, The Publishers Association

The main interest in the table lies in the way it highlights the importance of the Smith/Menzies combination in paperback sales and the significant showing of CTNs. In hardbacks, it comes as no surprise to find bookshops accounting for the bulk, though once again Smith/Menzies are a very significant factor.

In terms of value, the percentages in Table 31 provide a guide to the importance of the different types of outlet. Attention should be focussed in Table 31 on the Euromonitor estimates for 1982 which are a refinement on those presented in earlier years. The figures are reproduced in Table 36 with the percentages reworked as a proportion of the estimated retail book market.

Table 36

Estimated Retail Distribution of Books - 1982

	Retail Sales (£m)	Market Shares (%)
W.H. Smith	120	20
John Menzies	30	5
Other bookshops	210	34
CTN outlets	60	10
Book clubs	50	8
Variety, department stores	45	7
Direct mail	30	5
Supermarkets	12	2
Others	53	9
TOTAL	610	100

Source: The Book Report, 1983, Euromonitor Publications

W. H. Smith/J. Menzies and Bookshops

In comparing the percentages in the two tables, one note of warning should be sounded, in as much as Table 35 does not apparently include Direct Mail and Book Clubs, which together make up about 13 per cent of the retail book market by value. Subject to that qualification, it follows logically that the market shares of such groups as Smith/Menzies and the CTNs, where paperback sales predominate, should be significantly lower when the measure is one of value rather than of unit. Looking further at the role of W .H . Smith and John Menzies in book retailing, the growth of total retail selling space at the two chains is given in Table 37. The rate of growth at W.H. Smith over the whole period covered is 6.8 per cent, and at Menzies 13.7 per cent, the latter admittedly from a small base.

Table 37 serves to illustrate the expansionary policy of the two groups, within which framework, management has allocated selling space. With books, over a period of years the proportion of space tended to decline as a result of the further expansion and/or addition of new lines that fall into the Menzies terminology of 'indoor leisure' and include such varied products as tapes, videos, wool, home computers, toys and records. In relatively recent experience, however, the

41

trend appears to have been reversed. In the case of both W. H.
Smith and John Menzies this change is linked to a shift in the
emphasis in management accounts from turnover to profits. At
Menzies for instance, there is a close correlation between the
allocation of space and gross profit per square foot earned on
individual products.   With Menzies' modern stores being
equipped with interchangeable fittings, the results of the
annual reviews of performance can be rapidly reflected in the
allocation of space. Currently a larger proportion of space is
being given to traditional goods including books, partly so as
to accommodate the highly successful computer magazines and
computer books.

Table 37

UK Retail Selling Space - W. H. Smith, John Menzies

	W. H. Smith			John Menzies		
	Increase in space	% change	Space at year end	Increase in space	% change	Space at year end
(thousand sq ft)						
1982-83	39	+2.3	1,707	+35	+6.0	620
1981-82	61	+3.8	1,668	+25	+4.5	585
1980-81	71	+4.6	1,607	+40	+7.7	560
1979-80	108	+7.6	1,536	+50	+10.6	520
1978-79	77	+5.7	1,428	+45	+10.6	470
1977-78	64	+5.0	1,351	+35	+9.0	425
1976-77	170	+15.2	1,287	+15	+4.0	390
1975-76	72	+6.9	1,117	+100	+8.1	375
1974-75	98	+10.3	1,045	+80	+36.3	275
1973-74	96	+11.2	947	NA	+41.0	195

Note: The W. H. Smith figures do not include Bowes & Bowes
Source: Reports and Accounts. Partly estimated

Gross margins from book sales compare favourably with those
from many other goods. At W. H. Smith, book sales have been
described as among the most profitable elements in the group's
turnover. Recognition of this has come with a rise in the
allocation of space to books of 9.1 per cent in 1981-82 compared to an overall increase of retail selling space that year

of 3.8 per cent and a rise in the allocation of 2.9 per cent in 1982-83 against 2.3 per cent overall. In 1984, the expansion in space devoted to books will again be at a more rapid rate than the overall retail total as the programme of space reallocation encompasses other outlets. Further evidence of this enhanced commitment to books is provided by the 64 per cent increase in moneys spent on book promotion and advertising in 1983 to around £¾m and the further planned advance in 1984 to £1m.

For independent bookshops the most valuable source of information is the annual Charter Group economic survey issued by the Booksellers Association. The Charter Group, formed in 1964, consists currently of some 340 businesses, owning approximately 400 stockholding bookshops, who prepare annual returns for analysis. Table 38 covers a period of fifteen years during which the size of the sample completing the questionnaires has expanded significantly. Consequently, the absolute figures for sales cannot be regarded as a measure of growth.

Table 38

Charter Group of Bookselling Results

Year to March 31	1966-67	1971-72	1975-76	1977-78	1979-80	1980-81	1981-82
Total sales (£m)	20.4	38.2	114.2	149.7	162.1	168.6	202.1
(per cent)	100	100	100	100	100	100	100
of which							
retail books	50.9	49.4	54.7	53.9	54.8	60.1	57.0
other books*	16.2	14.9	16.9	15.2	12.9	12.8	11.0
other goods	32.9	35.7	28.4	30.9	32.3	27.1	32.0
Gross profit	25.6	25.4	27.9	28.9	29.1	29.2	29.4
less							
wages, salaries	13.0	12.7	14.7	15.1	15.7	16.8	15.9
rent, rates	2.3	2.7	3.5	3.6	3.7	3.9	4.7
other	5.9	6.6	6.4	7.1	6.9	6.6	8.0
Net trading profit	4.4	3.4	3.3	3.1	2.8	1.9	0.8

* sales to libraries, book agents, schools

The breakdown of sales shows some fluctuation from year to year but no trend in the division between sales of books and sales

43

of other goods. Within the book total, however, there has been a marked swing towards retail sales at the expense of institutional sales. For many booksellers, such a development will have had its silver lining in that institutional business, with its heavy administrative paperwork, can be relatively unprofitable unless the amount of such business is kept within limits.

The rise in gross margins from 25.6 per cent to 29.4 per cent is a reflection of the altered pattern of retail to institutional sales. It can also be taken as evidence that booksellers as a whole have had some success in widening the discounts received from publishers. If this is indeed the case, it is recognition of the increases in costs borne by booksellers. It comes despite the fact that the bookseller takes less of a stock risk than previously through the increasingly general practice of publishers granting 'see-safe' and return privileges.

Within the cost breakdown, the proportion of revenue taken by rent and rates has risen inexorably, illustrating a point made by Michael Pountney of W. H. Smith, namely that the key pressure on independent booksellers is the cost of occupation. This is driving bookshops out of the high street and away from prime locations for their business. While other costs absorb a much larger proportion of sales, they lend themselves to somewhat better control. Indeed, between 1966-67 and 1981-82, wages and salaries as a percentage of turnover rose by 22 per cent, 'other' costs by 36 per cent and rent and rates by 104 per cent. The net result has been the virtual evaporation of net trading margins from 4.4 per cent in 1966-67 to 0.8 per cent in 1981-82.

This apparently intolerable situation does, however, on analysis become somewhat less critical. It is relevant that the period to 31 March 1982 encompassed the exceptionally severe winter. Also, the percentages can occasionally be slightly distorted by variations in the sample. An analysis confined to 291 members of the Charter Group who reported in both 1981-82 and 1980-81 and whose circumstances had not materially changed between the two years reveals net margins of 1 per cent, compared to 2 per cent a year earlier. As far as 1982-83 and 1983-84 are concerned, once the figures become available they will certainly show an improvement on those for 1981-82. The point needs also to be made that the analysis of the financial performance of an industry which is very largely made up of small units - often of the 'momma and poppa' variety - is a much more difficult exercise than would be the case if all the constituents filed annual accounts at Companies House.

At the level of individual bookshops and specialist chains, a striking feature is the wide variation in the approach to present and future challenges.

This is epitomized on the one hand by the defensive attitude of those who appear haunted by the idea of resale price maintenance being eroded - let alone suppressed. Developments that

have attracted their wrath have included an offer by BPCC to
sell books from the group's publishing division to shareholders
at discounts of 25 per cent to 30 per cent, evidence that a
publisher was giving a university student union discounts to
which it was not entitled, the book clubs' use of premium
offers and, perhaps less surprisingly, the use of discounts by
publishers supplying direct to the final customer. At the same
time, the pages of The Bookseller also provide an encouraging
number of instances of enterprise on the part of booksellers,
small as well as large. One example is of the Yorkshire
bookshop that uses a trailer and tent to set up a shop at
weekend shows and displays, thereby going out to its public
rather than waiting for the public to come to it. And more
generally the advance in the membership of the Booksellers
Association from 2,800 in 1974 to 3,400 in 1983 may be
interpreted positively - although it no doubt reflects in part
a simple desire by retailers to be empowered to sell book
tokens.

Among the bookshops where management clearly has the most
outward looking, entrepreneurial attitudes, a number are members of specialist chains. It could be argued that the greater
financial security that this can bring helps make an entrepreneurial approach more of a practical possibility than might
otherwise have been the case. The gradual development of the
chains of bookshops in such groups as Associated Book
Publishers (Hammicks), W. H. Smith (Bowes & Bowes), Penguin,
Blackwells and Websters is undoubtedly significant. Even
Pentos's continued commitment to bookselling in the midst of
its problems can be interpreted as a sign of confidence. And in
terms of massive development plans, one of the most ambitious
is that of Joseph Causton in respect of Claude Gill which it
acquired in the summer of 1982. Over the next ten to fifteen
years investments of £10-20m are envisaged, with a view to
building Claude Gill into a nationwide bookshop chain; in addition, the existing shops are to be progressively refitted.
From abroad the Canadian chain, Classic Bookshops, announced
last October its forthcoming entry into the UK, starting with
an initial 10-15 shops planned for a chosen locality. In the
view of Mr Brian Melzack, whose chain includes 115 stores
throughout Canada, Britain is 'under-bookshopped'. This view is
shared by a number of UK publishers/bookshop owners and some
thought is being given to the development of franchise operations.

The paradox that profitless activity as portrayed in the
Charter Group results should coincide with a plethora of expansion plans and new developments is hard to explain. An optimistic view centres on the explosive interest in home computers
and the related software and computer books. Some booksellers
see the sale of the software and the computer books as an
exciting new activity and one, moreover, which may help them to
overcome the margin squeeze to which rising high street rents

45

subject them. Certainly the response to the setting up at the start of 1983 of Websters Software as wholesaler of computer books and software has been such as to justify the most optimistic estimates. The point has to be made, however, that by no means all bookshops have the space, staff and customers to justify branching into the computer world. Secondly, to the extent that international analogies have any validity, the rapid growth of bookshop chains in the USA (referred to at the end of the chapter on paperbacks) is also seen as an encouraging pointer. A third consideration revolves around the fact that retail bookshop proprietors may well feel more loved by publishers than was at one time the case, when the latter were entranced by the growth of alternative outlets.

Confectionery, Tobacco, Newsagents

The role of CTNs in book retailing may be glimpsed through the results of Websters book wholesaling subsidiary, Bookwise.

Table 39

Webster Group's Book Distribution Results

Year to 31 Dec.	Turnover	Trading Profit	Margins (%)
(£thousands)			
1982	32,040	1,177	3.7
1981	30,002	1,251	4.2
1980	24,627	705	2.9
1979	21,057	384	1.8
1978	17,906	622	3.5
1977	16,394	809	4.9
1976	9,748	534	5.5
1975	6,892	314	4.6
1974	4,692	239	5.1

Source: Report and Accounts of Websters Group

Bookwise's chief customers are the CTN chains and other retail chains such as Debenhams, Boots, Woolworths and Asda. Their main role is that of wholesalers of paperbacks where the 30 million books they distribute in any one year account for about

a quarter of the mass-market paperback market and the great majority of the CTN market for such paperbacks.

In the period 1974-82, Bookwise's turnover rose by 582 per cent; this compares with an advance in industry sales of hardbacks and paperbacks of 186 per cent (Table 59) and an increase in industry paperback sales of 254 per cent.

While Bookwise's performance must reflect in part its success in increasing market share, it also undoubtedly mirrors the expanding role of books (chiefly paperbacks) in CTNs during this period, notably in the mid-1970s. Looking more closely at the table, one feature has been the slowdown in sales in 1982; this persisted in 1983, when little real growth occurred in sales of mass-market paperbacks. Undoubtedly, the recession had a particularly adverse impact on book buying - largely impulse - in CTNs whose customers are typically in the lower socio economic groupings. While this is a cyclical phenomenon, the weakness is being perhaps magnified by more structural changes. One of these concerns the challenge to book buying at this socioeconomic level that is presented by calls on disposable income from rival and more glamorous products. Another is the damage done to the CTN purchaser of past over-production of cheap titles that were bought on a promise they did not fulfil. This is prompting a number of CTN chains to re-examine their strategy. In books, it means preserving the value for money appeal and at the same time edging away from the lower end of the market in respect of titles that are not in the blockbuster class, the so-called middle list.

NSS Newsagents is an instance of a group where opportunities still clearly exist. The chain consists of 500 stores virtually all of which carry paperbacks and children's hardbacks; the smaller stores, numbering some 200, only carry hardbacks over the Christmas season. Adult hardbacks carried by the larger stores include Bounty Books, which emphasize value for money. Looking some five to ten years ahead, management sees the news and magazine side remaining strong and confectionery holding up but with greater emphasis on health foods and other more specialized products. One sector that is clearly in decline is cigarettes and tobacco. This leaves stationery, greetings cards, books and toys all of which are currently of approximately the same importance. One of them is expected to develop into a fourth major area of activity. In this connection the trend towards larger units is important since it makes bookselling a physical possibility in an increasing number of NSS (and other CTN) shops.

At Martin the Newsagent, book sales throughout the 500 branches amounted to some £14m in 1982-83 and represented about 10 per cent of group turnover. Some 60 per cent was paperback and 40 per cent was hardback. Book sales have been on a rising curve in recent years and management's view is that books remain a desirable and profitable line and one that justifies further development. The mix may well, however, be different from that which made economic sense in the 1970s. In particular, one may anticipate some movement towards a wider range of choice in the larger units, while at the same time, sales of traditional mass-market paperbacks could well remain relatively subdued.

Throughout these shifts in demand and changes of emphasis one feature that remains unaltered is the public's concern with expense. A further manifestation is in the development of the remainder business.

Remainder Bookshops

The remainder market, at retail prices, is estimated to have approached £12m in 1982. This calculation is made in the Euromonitor Book Report, 1983. In Table 31 remainder bookshop sales are included in the 'other bookshops' classification.

If one accepts the figure of £12m, such sales represent 2 per cent of the UK market for books. By comparison, book discounting has been estimated at 2 per cent of total book sales in Australia (Business Review Weekly, letter to the editor, M. G. Zifcak, August 1982). In the USA, a recent Gallup survey indicated that as much as 22 per cent of books purchased in November/December 1983 were bought at a discounted price (31 per cent of hardcovers and 18 per cent of paperbacks). No doubt, the absence of resale price maintenance has something to do with the American experience, though it would not appear to have had much influence in Australia.

In the UK the rapid growth in sales of remainders dates from the mid-1970s with the development of such groups as Words and Music, BSC Remainders (the Booksmith chain of shops) and Susan Reynolds Books. Susan Reynolds was formed in November 1977, the first unit being a 400 sq ft shop in Acton, West London, secured on a short lease at £100 a week covering the Christmas period. The initial stock consisted of 5,000 copies of twenty titles, fiction and non-fiction, purchased at 7½p per book, which went on sale at a uniform price of 30p.

The sources of remainders have typically included both the USA and the UK. In the case of the USA, imports of certain titles have led occasionally to accusations of copyright infringement: the US rights on a UK title having been sold, the US edition may subsequently be remaindered and copies imported into the UK before any remaindering of the UK edition. A celebrated case involved the publishers Calder & Boyars and Words and Music in 1966. The latter was discovered to be selling several US paperback editions of Calder titles.

Remainder chains occasionally enjoy direct contact with publishers through 'put' deals. Booksmith, for example, will contract to purchase the unsolds up to a certain level on one or more titles at an agreed price after an agreed lapse of time

following original publication. Under such arrangements, the UK remainder wholesaler, who has been the main source of product, is bypassed.

The business of remainders is changing, and this is best illustrated in the rise and fall of the Susan Reynolds chain which achieved sales in the year to November, 1981 of £3.4m with pre-tax profits of £190,000 and yet in January 1984 called in the receiver.

At the same time as the company grew in size, so did its appetite for books. It then found that one source of inexpensive, good quality titles from the USA was shrinking with the steep rise of the dollar. Price inflation also started to have an effect on UK remainders, the asking price for which changed from say 10p to 35p. Management responded by edging up-market. The formula of tail-end leases of high street shops was modified to the extent that, of the twenty outlets making up the Susan Reynolds chain, two-thirds fell into that category and one-third was made up of 'permanent' shops. The average size was some 1,800 sq ft. Also, the single price for all products had given way to up to six different prices - 50p, £1.50, £2.00, £3.00, £4.00, £5.00 and (exceptionally) £10.00. Susan Reynolds for its part started to develop a new source of product through the publication of books bearing the Susan Reynolds imprint. Examples in 1982 included four titles that represented re-marketed sections of Orbis Books' partwork, The Movie, each retailing at £1.50.

Changing its spots did not however succeed and the receiver was called into a company which had acquired overheads (high street rents and rates) and was short of product. For remainder bookshops as a whole the sales explosion had come to an end in 1982. Apart from the loss of the exceptionally favourable opportunities that they had enjoyed when the pound was overvalued, they also suffered from the fact that the recession, as already noted, was felt particularly keenly at the lower end of the market.

Comment

In reviewing this section on distribution, one fairly general impression is that books are in a relatively good position to compete with other products for shelf space. They do not suffer from any major prejudices at the retail end and they offer the retailer satisfactory gross margins. The judgement of the ultimate consumer can, of course, negate these advantages.

In the post-war period a significant point that emerges is the number of changes that have occurred, the main effect of which has been to hold back price rises to the ultimate purchaser. This comment may strike a discordant note when set against the criticisms that rising book prices have attracted, and the frequently expressed view that books now cost much too much. It remains true, nonetheless, that 'bargain tables' are now a regular feature of bookshops, that remainder bookshops have grown from virtually nothing ten years ago to perhaps 2 per cent of the non-institutional domestic book market and that simultaneous book clubs offer a large number of book buyers important savings. More generally, these developments have no doubt helped take some of the wind out of the sails of the RPM-abolition lobby.

In common with most industries, the financial squeeze of recent years has led to a cutback of retail stocks, which must have harmed sales, though the extent of 'lost' business is impossible to establish. However, the calamitous financial state of bookselling, as depicted in the analyses of the Charter Group of Booksellers, does not appear to have had a major impact on the population of establishments selling books. It is true, however, that this overall stability hides some changes, with the larger establishments, notably the big retail chains and the bookselling groups, increasing their numbers of outlets while some of the smaller units have disappeared from the high streets or have disappeared altogether.

Looking ahead, in terms of booksellers' mix of business, the reduction noted earlier in the contribution from institutional business seems more likely to persist. This may stem in part from the emergence of powerful, competing, library supply groups such as John Menzies, from developments of the kind that the Yorkshire Purchasing Organisation is encouraging, and, more generally, from a recognition that the rewards are simply insufficiently attractive.

Taking up again the question of size, one of the more intriguing developments over the last two years or so is the evidence that the larger groups involved in bookselling are sufficiently optimistic to want to invest additional funds. This is true of W. H. Smith which is expanding its book space and increasing its promotion outlays. Joseph Causton is intent on committing millions of pounds to the further development of the Claude Gill chain. Foreign investment represented by Classic Bookshops of Canada is planning an ambitious entry into the industry. And other examples exist.

At the same time, another developing feature of bookselling appears to be reduced emphasis on mass-market paperbacks, particularly relevant to CTNs, offset by strength in the book ranges of the more traditional book outlets. And in terms of the more modern products, those related to the home computer are seen as having interesting potential.

For the specialist bookshop owner intent on profiting from these trends, the question of capital may well be a problem. One solution could lead to the formation of new chains and associations of bookshops, possibly under publishing umbrellas. From the point of view of publishers, the present pattern of distribution presents a picture of greater variety than previously, which in turn throws up opportunities that had not

50

existed before - an example at one end of the scale being 'put' deals with remainder bookshops.

Within the chains, the steady expansion noted earlier in the average size of retail units is undoubtedly important to bookselling, offering display opportunities leading to the formation of small book departments in such stores. The strengthening of library supply as a result of John Menzies investments is also a positive development, particularly in relation to exports.

Apart from maximizing the opportunities presented by the retail trade, publishers also have the option of themselves selling directly to the ultimate customer or engaging in special sales such as premiums. Up to now, many have avoided doing so on any scale, on the reasonable grounds that this would undermine the book trade, which is overwhelmingly their major outlet. This policy should no doubt continue to be in the self-interest of most publishers. However, a trend of the kind discussed earlier towards chains and away from the independent bookshop undoubtedly weakens the distribution system for the more specialized title. If such titles are still to be published, such a gap needs to be filled - most probably by the publisher, aided perhaps by the wholesaler.

Finally, the point has to be made that the whole of this discussion has been predicated on the continuance of resale price maintenance. Were it to be outlawed under EEC regulations, there is a belief that is close to being universally held in the trade, that this would damage considerably the existing pattern of UK book distribution. The evidence from the Australian experience does not, in fact, justify such extreme fears, and in particular the abolition of RPM in Australia has not prevented the development of many Australian-interest lists, which have specialist appeal. International comparisons could, however, prove misleading.

THE USA

1. US Population Trends

The population trends presented in Table 40 point up:
(a) the decline that took place in the 1970s in that part of
    the population that goes to the educational establishment
    - very broadly defined, the 0-21-year-olds,
(b) the rise in that part that forms the labour force, the
    22-64-year-olds, and
(c) the rise in the elderly, the 65-year-olds and over.
Within these broad categories, the number of 5-13-year-olds
fell by 6.3m or 17 per cent between 1970 and 1980, while the
22-34-year-olds increased by 13.5m or 38 per cent.

Table 40

US Population Trends

(thousands)	1970	1975	1980	1985	1990	2000
Under 5	17,148	15,882	16,024	18,803	19,437	17,852
5-13	36,636	33,440	30,301	29,098	32,568	35,080
14-17	15,910	16,934	15,810	14,392	12,771	16,045
18-21	14,707	16,484	17,167	15,442	14,507	14,990
0-21 sub total	84,401	82,740	79,302	77,735	79,283	83,967
22-34	35,274	42,038	48,761	52,270	51,728	44,113
35-44	23,142	22,815	25,837	31,376	36,592	41,344
45-54	23,310	23,768	22,749	22,457	25,311	35,875
55-64	18,664	19,774	21,250	21,737	20,776	23,257
22-64 sub total	100,390	108,395	118,597	127,840	134,407	144,589
65+	20,087	22,405	25,221	27,305	29,824	31,822
TOTAL	204,878	213,540	223,120	232,880	243,514	260,378

Notes: Due to rounding, there are some slight discrepancies in the
totals. In the interest of consistency, the detailed projections
published in 1979 have been used.
Source: US Bureau of the Census

The projections for the 1980s indicate no change in the overall rate of population growth, with a compound rate of increase in the period 1980-90 of 0.9 per cent being identical to the rate achieved between 1970 and 1980. Within the 0-21-year-olds, the main difference is a sharp reversal in the downward trend in the 0-5-year-olds which are shown increasing by over 2.8m between 1980 and 1985; this will have worked its way through to the 5-13-year-olds by 1985 with a reversal of the downward trend there emerging in the period 1985 to 1990.

Table 41

US Population Changes 1970 to 1990

	1970 to 1975	1975 to 1980	(1970 to 1980)	1980 to 1985	1985 to 1990	(1980 to 1990)	(1990 to 2000)
(thousands)							
Under 5	-1,266	+142	-1,124	+2,779	+634	+3,413	-1,585
5-13	-3,196	-3,139	-6,335	-1,203	+3,470	+2,267	+2,512
14-17	+1,024	-1,124	-100	-1,418	-1,621	-3,039	+3,274
18-21	+1,777	+ 683	+2,460	-1,725	-935	-2,660	+483
0-21 sub total	-1,661	-3,438	-5,099	-1,567	+1,548	-19	+4,684
22-34	+6,764	+6,723	+13,487	+3,509	-542	+2,967	-7,615
35-44	-327	+3,022	+2,695	+5,539	+5,216	+10,755	+4,752
45-54	+458	-1,019	-561	-292	+2,854	+2,562	+10,564
55-64	+1,110	+1,476	+2,586	+487	-961	-474	+2,481
22-64 sub total	+8,005	+10,202	+18,207	+9,243	+6,567	+15,810	+10,182
65+	+2,318	+2,816	+5,134	+2,084	+2,519	+4,603	+1,998
TOTAL	+8,662	+9,580	+18,242	+9,760	+10,634	+20,394	+16,864

Source: US Bureau of the Census

In the 22-64-year-old band, the 22-34-year-olds will continue growing in the 1980s but at a slower pace, the absolute increase between 1980 and 1990 being 2.9m. This masks, however, contrasting trends with the 22-24-year-olds contracting by 1.8m and the 25-34-year-olds increasing by 4.7m. The 35-44-year-olds on the other hand, are due to experience a rise of as much as

10¾m; this works through to the 45-54 age bracket in the decade to the year 2,000. Finally, the elderly remain an area of continuing population expansion.

As in a number of other countries during the 1980s, demographic trends in the United States will favour those supplying the adult working population and the elderly rather than those supplying the educational band. However, by the end of the decade renewed expansion in the school-age market will occur, starting at the elementary levels and extending into the secondary school population in the 1990s. College enrolments by 1990 are expected to be some 11m against 11.6m in 1980.

2. US Book Publishing Statistics

The overall rate of growth of US publishers' sales in the period 1963-82 has been 8.7 per cent. This compares with a rate of inflation as measured by the consumer price index of 6.2 per cent, indicating a real rate of growth in US publishers' sales of some 2.5 per cent. Since 1972 publishers' sales have expanded at 10.6 per cent against an inflation rate of 8.7 per cent, while in more recent experience publishers' sales have by this measure done no more than match inflation: between 1977 and 1982 the compound rate of increase in the industry's sales of 9.9 per cent (10.1 per cent if the estimates for audiovisual and standardized tests are excluded) was in line with a rate of increase in the consumer price index of 9.7 per cent. However, if one takes units sold, there was a rise from 1,653m in 1977 to 1,922m in 1982, indicating a compound rate of growth of 3.1 per cent and, therefore, a rather healthier underlying situation.

The years covered in Tables 42 and 43 have been divided into five periods of four to five years so as to illustrate relative rates of change. The sectors that have consistently outperformed the average for the industry have been adult trade books, professional titles and mass-market paperbacks. The consistent underperformer has been subscription reference books. Sales of elementary and secondary textbooks and juvenile trade books have expanded at a below-average rate since 1967.

The sales performance of the US publishing industry during the recent recession (Table 44) proved to be stronger than many might have anticipated and certainly more resilient than many industry spokesmen's comments would have led one to expect. Table 44 shows a rise of 1.6 per cent in unit sales in 1982, and a 5.2 per cent advance in the value of sales. The strength of unit sales owes much to a somewhat surprising 5.4 per cent advance in mass-market paperbacks. A separate analysis of consumer expenditure on books highlights the sluggishness of the institutional market (libraries and institutions) where sales in 1982, although up 10 per cent by value over 1981, were down

Table 42

Estimated US Publishers' Sales

(US$million)	Old Series			New Series						
	1963	1967	1972	1972	1977	1978	1979	1980	1981	1982
Trade	230	353	490	442	832	984	1,045	1,273	1,428	1,434
Adult	126	188	353	331	670	799	854	1,044	1,180	1,176
Juvenile	104	165	137	111	162	185	191	229	248	258
Religion	81	108	130	118	251	279	301	325	353	383
Professional	166	237	381	381	698	805	885	1,006	1,120	1,242
Law, business	73	94	187	192	286	333	370	429	483	NA
Medicine	24	38	57	57	163	194	214	242	254	NA
Technical, Science	69	105	137	132	249	278	301	335	383	NA
Book clubs	143	180	356	241	407	463	502	534	566	582
Mail order	NA	NA	NA	199	396	440	486	563	657	580
Mass-market paperbacks*	87	130	253	253	543	609	676	761	882	998
Rack-sized	87	130	253	250	488	544	603	653	736	843E
non-rack-sized	NA	NA	NA	3	55	65	73	108	146	155E

University presses	18	31	41	41	56	62	68	78	81	90
Elementary & secondary texts	305	421	498	498	756	833	930	952	1,013	1,069
College texts	160	287	375	375	650	737	826	953	1,073	1,180
Subscription, reference	381	441	279	279	294	341	384	349	355	360
Sub total	1,571	2,188	2,803	2,827	4,883	5,553	6,103	6,794	7,528	7,918*
Audiovisual	NA	NA	NA	116	151	151	146	167	167	170E
Standardized tests	13	22	27	27	45	52	62	67	73	75E
Other	102+	110+	177+	49	63	52	57	67	75	80E
TOTAL ($million)	1,686	2,320	3,007	3,019	5,142	5,808	6,368	7,095	7,843	8,243E
TOTAL (million units)	NA	NA	NA	NA	1,653	1,733	1,754	1,860	1,892	1,922

E Estimated.
+ Including audiovisual and mail order publications.
* The total shown in the summary table of Book Industry Trends, 1983 is $7,792,000,000, the constituents add up to $7,918,000,000 as here.
Sources: Association of American Publishers, published in Publishers Weekly, Book Industry Trends, 1983, Book Industry Study Group Inc.

5.7 per cent in unit terms. Direct sales to consumers, which include the mail order and subscription reference sections,

Table 43

Rates of Change of US Publishers' Sales 1963 to 1982

	1963 to 1967	1967 to 1972	1972 to 1977	1977 to 1982	1963 to 1982
(per cent)					
Trade	+11.3	+6.8	+13.5	+11.5	+10.2
Adult	+10.5	+13.4	+15.1	+11.9	+12.5
Juvenile	+12.2	-3.7	+7.8	+9.8	+4.9
Religion	+7.5	+3.8	+16.3	+8.8	+8.5
Professional	+9.3	+9.9	+12.9	+12.2	+11.2
Law, business	+6.5	+14.8	+8.3	+14.0+	+11.1+
Medicine	+12.2	+8.5	+23.4	+11.7+	+14.0+
Technical, Science	+11.1	+5.5	+13.5	+11.4+	+10.0+
Book clubs	+5.9	+14.6	+11.0	+7.5	+7.7
Mail order	NA	NA	+14.7	+7.9	NA
Mass-market paperbacks	+10.6	+14.3	+16.5	+12.9	+13.7
Rack-sized	+10.6	+14.3	+14.3	+11.6	+12.7
Non-rack-sized	–	–	+78.9	+23.0	NA
University presses	+14.5	+5.8	+6.4	+9.9	+8.9
Elementary & secondary texts	+8.4	+3.4	+8.7	+7.2	+6.8
College texts	+15.7	+5.5	+11.6	+12.7	+11.1
Subscription, reference	+3.7	-8.8	+1.0	+4.1	-0.3
Sub total	+8.6	+5.1	+11.6	+10.1	+8.9
Audiovisual	NA	NA	+5.4	+2.3E	NA
Standardized tests	+14.1	+4.2	+10.7	+10.8E	+9.7E
Other	NA	NA	+5.1	+4.8	NA
TOTAL ($million)	+8.3	+5.3	+11.3	+9.9	+8.7
TOTAL (million units)	NA	NA	NA	+3.1	NA

+ Period to 1981   E Estimated
Source: Association of American Publishers, published in Publishers Weekly, Book Industry Study Trends, 1983, Book Industry Study Group Inc.

were an area of marked weakness, recording drops of 0.6 per cent and 10 per cent in value and volume terms respectively against a year earlier.

The evidence of 1983 points to a cyclical recovery with publishers' net book sales by value rising 10.9 per cent in the first nine months over a year earlier and in terms of units by 4 per cent. There was, moreover, a marked acceleration during the year with third quarter sales up 16.3 per cent by value and 9.1 per cent by volume.

Table 44

US Publishers Sales 1981 and 1982

	1981 ($m)	change %	1982* ($m)	1981 (m units)	change %	1982* (m units)
Trade	1,428	+0.4	1,434	436	-0.5	434
Adult	1,180	-0.3	1,176	301	-1.7	296
Juvenile	248	+4.0	258	135	+2.2	138
Religion	353	+8.5	383	104	+2.9	107
Professional	1,120	+10.9	1,242	63	+1.6	64
Law, business	483		NA			
Medicine	254		NA			
Technical, Science	383		NA			
Book clubs	566	+2.8	582	214	-2.8	208
Mail order	657	-11.7	580	61	-11.5	54
Mass-market paperbacks	882	+13.2	998	634	+5.4	668
Rack-sized	736	+14.5	843	NA		NA
Non-rack-sized	146	+6.2	155	NA		NA
University presses	81	+11.1	90	12	+8.3	13
Elhi texts	1,013	+5.5	1,069	258	+1.6	262
College texts	1,073	+10.0	1,180	110	+0.9	111
Subscription, reference	355	+1.4	360	1	0	1
TOTAL	7,528	+5.2	7,918	1,892	+1.6	1,922

Source: Association of American Publishers, published in Publishers Weekly; Book Industry Study Trends, 1983, Book Industry Study Group

Over the full three quarters, sales of trade books advanced the most rapidly - up 19 per cent in value 13.8 per cent in units - and strong performances were put up by professional titles (up 12.3 per cent and up 6.5 per cent) and mass-market publications (up 14.3 per cent and up 5.0 per cent). Book club sales, Elhi textbooks and mail order publications remained flat, recording actual declines in unit terms.

Table 45

Estimated US Publishers' Sales to 1987

	1977 ($m)	Value Annual rate of change per cent 1977-82	1982 ($m)	Value Annual rate of change per cent 1982-87	1987 ($m)	Units Annual rate of change per cent 1982-87
Trade	832	+11.5	1,434	+13.4	2,684	+9.4
Religion	251	+8.8	383	+12.2	681	+7.1
Professional	698	+12.2	1,242	+14.0	2,388	+4.2
Book clubs	407	+7.5	582	+7.5	837	+1.9
Mail order	396	+7.9	580	+13.1	1,072	+11.2
Mass-market paperbacks	543	+12.9	998	+16.8	2,170	+9.1
University presses	56	+9.9	90	+11.2	153	+8.6
Elementary & secondary texts	756	+7.2	1,069	+8.2	1,587	+3.2
College texts	650	+12.7	1,180	+10.6	1,953	+0.9
Subscription, reference	294	+4.1	360	+4.0	438	+2.6
TOTAL	4,883	+10.1	7,918	+12.0	13,963	+7.1

Note: Mass-market paperbacks include non-rack sized paperbacks
Source: Book Industry Trends, 1982, John P. Dessauer, Book Industry Study Group; Publishers Weekly; Quarterly Statistics, The Publishers Association

A longer perspective of sales trends is provided in Table 45, which presents forecasts through to 1987, prepared by John Dessauer. These suggest a distinct acceleration in the five-year period 1982-87, compared to the five years 1977-82 in terms of units and value. Above-average growth is anticipated in mail order, professional books (value only), trade titles and mass-market paperbacks. Below-average growth is forecast for subscription reference books, continuing a trend of long duration, school books, college texts and book clubs.

3. British Presence in the USA

The post-war history of British publishing is rich with instances that illustrate the fact that the American market is full of pitfalls. Some relatively recent examples include Collins's purchase in 1974 of the World Publishing Company. The rationale behind the acquisition was that the merger of World's bible interests with Collins's existing bible business in the USA would create an economically viable unit, and in addition the US publishing base would be usefully broadened through the addition of World's children's and reference books divisions. After sustaining heavy losses for a number of years, these interests were disposed of in 1979; terminal costs were some £850,000.

Associated Book Publishers embarked in the mid-1970s on a three-pronged attack on the American market involving the development of lists in the fields of: (a) adult trade books, (b) children's books, and (c) academic, scientific and technical books. After incurring substantial operating losses, the decision was taken in 1980 to restrict the American effort to the academic, scientific and technical lists.

W. H. Smith launched itself in 1978 into an ambitious programme, which involved US distribution for UK houses based on its own US warehouse distribution centre and sales force. In subsequent years, a number of publishing businesses were acquired including a trade publishing imprint (Windward), a publisher of books for remainder merchants (Sun Flower) and a small religious publisher (Crossroads). After incurring substantial losses, in November 1981 it was announced that the company would be discontinuing contract distribution and general publishing and would be concentrating on the remainder/bargain book business and on religious publishing. In 1983 the religious publisher, Crossroads, was the object of a management buy-out.

In looking more widely at the links that UK firms have in the United States, a point that emerges is the considerable variety that exists. At one extreme, there is the UK firm that aims to sell the North American rights on its UK titles (where such rights have not been separately sold). This accounts for the great bulk of British publishing.

A firm such as Hamlyn actively sells both rights and co-editions to a wide range of American publishers including St

Martin's Press of Macmillans, Rand McNally and Facts on File.
Many co-editions of popular general interest titles are
published with Crown Publishers who also distribute some Hamlyn
titles through their promotional company outlet. Hamlyn also do
business with a number of other promotional houses and annual
turnover comes to just under £2 million.

A more direct involvement comes through the use of a specialist US firm, such as Merrimack, which will organize the
warehousing, distribution and selling for UK firms. Merrimack
receives books on consignment from the UK publishers; the
latter pay the cost of shipment to the USA as well as a pro
rata share of marketing and warehouse expenses. In many instances, as is the case, for example, with the UK imprints owned by
International Thomson, the UK publisher sells the US rights for
its big authors and uses Merrimack for the rest.

In the past, Merrimack has been used by Hutchinson and Faber
& Faber among other UK houses. Following the establishment of
their own company in the USA, Faber & Faber transferred the
warehousing and distribution to Harper & Row and on the sales
side appointed their own head of marketing. One of his tasks
is to control sales through Faber & Faber's membership of
selected groups of commission sales teams. It is hoped that the
present turnover of £1m can be boosted through membership in
the groups that are best suited to Faber & Faber's list, with
its academic strengths, and as a result of their having somebody who permanently champions their interests. The
Americanization of Faber & Faber Inc. was taken a step further
with the appointment in 1983 of their first American editor.
The US company now has three roles:
(a) as an export outlet for the parent company's titles,
(b) as a source of indigenous publishing with about four titles
    planned in each of the next two years, and
(c) as a purchaser of the US rights of books published by Faber
    & Faber but where the parent company does not control such
    rights.
A recent instance of (c) concerns a title of Tom Stoppard's
where the author and his agent clearly preferred to stay with
Faber & Faber in the expectation that the small size of Faber's
US operation would ensure maximum support. The convenience factor of dealing with one firm, well known to the author, will no
doubt have also influenced the decision.

Routledge & Kegan Paul are an illustration of a firm that has
long maintained a direct presence in the USA. They opened their
US office in Boston in 1971, since when it has been gradually
built up to its present size of eleven staff. Under the US
company's director of American operations there is one person
in charge of sales/promotion, four others who cover such mat-
ters as the preparation of promotional material and attendances
at conferences and five involved on order processing and
accounts. Warehousing and distribution are now done by the US
firm, Mercedes Inc. of Brooklyn.

The US business is heavily oriented towards institutions, being about 60 per cent to libraries (chiefly academic titles), 20 per cent to colleges, and 20 per cent trade. Under a Routledge & Kegan Paul Book Scheme, bookshops who guarantee to have in stock selected Routledge & Kegan Paul titles receive special discounts. Sales have typically been based on the use of commission salesmen. Increasingly, however, Routledge have been doing their own representation in bookstores. In an important recent development, since June 1982 Routledge have their own US acquisition editor, who is responsible for an active publishing programme in the area of public policy, for sale primarily in the USA. The appointment was seen as a means of 'energizing' the effective marketing of the whole list. In the year to 31 March 1983, exports to the 'Americas' (including therefore Canada) came to £1,089,000, which represented 48 per cent of total exports and 21 per cent of total turnover.

Turning to instances of UK firms whose existing US business is at least partly the result of acquisition, Viking Penguin is an important example. Control was bought by the Pearson Group in 1975. In the annual report that year, after an enumeration of the merits of The Viking Press, it was said that 'this purchase establishes in New York a means of increasing substantially the sale of Penguins in the United States and should create in four or five years a publishing base there comparable to the Penguin operation in the United Kingdom. The old, rigid distinctions between hardcover and paperback publishing are becoming obsolete. Penguin and Viking will be able to publish every kind of book for their markets, in any appropriate form or shape, for sale virtually throughout the world.'

In the light of these ambitions it may be of interest to take stock of what has happened in the intervening eight years. Turnover in 1982 amounted to $31.4m (compared to $28.5m in 1981 and $19m in 1978), and pre-tax profits amounted to $2.0m (as against $0.85m in 1981 and a loss in 1978). Currently, somewhat more than 60 per cent of revenue comes from the Penguin paperback side and rather less than 40 per cent from the Viking hardback side. In 1979, when Viking came under full management control of the Penguin Group, the proportions were roughly equal. The change reflects a doubling in Penguin revenue over the last three years and a rise of 36 per cent in the number of units sold. Titles published number about 200 a year for Penguin and 100 for Viking.

Running in tandem such a hardback and a paperback operation has clearly presented some special challenges. Indeed, since the purchase of Viking, the profits performance has been disappointing and several management reorganizations have taken place. Probably the most significant is that which occurred in 1983-84 following the resignation in September, 1983 of Irving Goodman, president and chief executive officer, and the assumption by Peter Mayer, chief executive of the whole Penguin Group, of day to day control of Viking Penguin as executive chairman. The appointment in January, 1984 of Alan Kellock as the new president and chief operating officer, together with a wide range of other senior appointments, marks the culmination of this latest reorganization.

The key to the recent changes lies in the dismantling of many of the elements that separated Penguin and Viking. This has meant the unification under a single management for publishing, editorial and marketing of the adult hardcover and the adult paperback divisions under the Viking and Penguin imprints respectively.

On the adult side, a merged editorial staff under Kathryn Court (formerly the Penguin US editor-in-chief) has been established, with all editors now functioning as Viking Penguin editors, some working more on originals, some more on take-overs, and some on both according to their talents and the merged company's needs. The launch of Elisabeth Sifton Books, a new editorial imprint, was announced early in 1984, with the first books to be published by Viking in the Autumn of 1984; Sifton, previously editor-in-chief of Viking, will acquire new books for both hardcover and paperback publication. She will have editorial autonomy and operate under a separate budget. Children's books (in cloth and paper) remain a separate editorial unit within this new merged structure.

The formal reorganization has been to a certain extent fore-shadowed by a number of measures taken earlier to simplify and increase the editorial links between the hardback and paperback sides. In that connection, the Viking trade paperback imprint, Compass, and Viking's children's imprint, Seafarer, had earlier been transferred to Penguin. Currently, about one third of Viking's new titles represent joint purchases with Penguin.

In a broader context, a developing feature of the Penguin Group is the extent to which titles are exchanged between the UK, the Australian, the US and other publishing centres. The way in which the Frederick Warne acquisition made by Penguin Publishing in July, 1983, is being developed throughout the whole Group, including the USA, is an instance of international coordination. However, the considerable degree of editorial autonomy that the different Penguin publishing offices enjoy is illustrated in the fact that Viking Penguin chose not to acquire the US rights to Audrey Eyton's bestseller The F-Plan, a title with which Penguin achieved sales records in such over-seas markets as Australia and New Zealand. The US rights were purchased by Crown and Bantam who successfully published it in the USA and Canada. With hindsight, this must be regarded as a missed opportunity. What may be of longer term significance is the purchase by Dell of Puffin's Fighting Fantasy series, of which Puffin in the UK has sold over a million in the first year.

In terms of distribution, Viking and Penguin already share a central warehouse. On the sales side, there is a sales director who oversees both paperback and hardback sales; this involves eighteen representatives, two of them academic specialists covering Viking and Penguin titles and sixteen who form a trade sales force carrying both imprints across a wide range of retail and wholesale book outlets. A characteristic of the sales effort has been the steady extension of the outlets into which Penguin and Viking titles are sold. At one time, for example, Penguin was seen essentially as a trade paperback house with an academic audience. Increasingly, Penguin has been establishing itself in the full range of outlets for trade books, as well as some mass-market outlets. The present editorial profile of Viking Penguin Inc. is such, however, that a combination of paperback and hardback sales is appropriate. Were the Penguin side to develop more than is the case at present into mass-market paperbacks a separation of sales functions might be called for.

In the Penguin Group's longer term plans, the American market occupies a major position, one important consideration being that Penguin's existing market share is not a hindrance to future growth in the way that it is in some of their traditional areas of operation. The paperback list will increase from 200 to 300 titles in 1984. Also, the increased emphasis on hardcover publishing which is characteristic of the Penguin Group as a whole will lead to a major increase in new Viking titles from 100 to 150 in 1985. More generally, Peter Mayer now sees Viking Penguin as having 'a progressive structure not only to acquire the right books, but just as importantly to decide in complete freedom how to publish each one with regard to format, price, market and the distribution channels to reach that market'. This carries interesting overtones of the 1975 'prospectus' quoted at the start of this section, the two major contrasts being the very much more modest scale of operations achieved so far compared to what was envisaged in 1975 and the extended time scale. But if, as seems likely, the Viking-Penguin merger is beginning to come right in terms of 'fit', the point has to be made that the re-structuring of the Pearson empire in the intervening period now provides constituents in the S. Pearson Group with access to financial resources that they did not previously have both for internal development and outside acquisition. The ambitious targets expressed in 1975 remain intact.

Another example of a publisher who has accepted that more haste often means less speed is provided by Associated Book Publishers. As noted earlier, ABP are now concentrating almost entirely on their scientific and academic lists, where they publish in the USA between 100 and 120 new titles a year. In this connection, UK editorial staff spend a good deal of time in the US commissioning titles from American authors; such titles can be said to originate in the UK and publication takes place in both countries. The year 1983 has, however, been important for Methuen Inc., ABP's US subsidiary, since it marked an important step in the development of the American company with the recruitment of their first resident US scientific editor. His task is to build a local list and the first title was published in 1983. Somewhat more than three-fifths of the list is academic and somewhat less than two-fifths is scientific. Production is handled in the UK; with the number of US authors increasing, the amount of US manufacturing has also risen, in direct response to the need for US production so that US authors may secure US copyright protection. As in the case of Faber & Faber noted earlier, sales are achieved in part through the use of groups of sales commission representatives who visit campuses and bookstores. In addition to their own order processing and administrative staff, ABP themselves employ seven people in marketing, publicity and promotion. Much of their work consists of the preparation of mailing shots, which are sent out on lists that are rented. While ABP's limited market share means that the flat college enrolment figures throughout the 1980s need not act as a significant brake on their performance, they can draw some comfort from the fact that the numbers of those in graduate study may well be sustained. The group's strategy, furthermore, is to avoid head-on conflict with US publishers and to emphasize areas that are relatively neglected and which coincide with existing editorial strengths at ABP; one such area is geography at the post-graduate level. ABP sees their US subsidiary as essential to their credibility in international academic and scientific publishing which demands world-wide marketing as well as editorial capability. Within five years they would hope to have achieved in the USA a medium-sized publishing position in their chosen sectors.

The two UK publishing houses that are undoubtedly making the biggest investments in North America are International Thomson Organisation (strictly speaking a Canadian house, but the money comes from the UK side of the North Sea and it only acquired Canadian domicile in 1978) and Longman. Both companies are expanding through acquisitions and organically, and both reflect the widely held view that it is the professional market that has some of the more attractive growth prospects.

In the case of Thomson, the main area of growth has been 'information technology', broadly defined. Since 1979, specific purchases in the USA have included:
(a) Wadsworth, the college publishers, for £16.2m (including long-term debt of £10.2m),
(b) Callaghan & Co., legal publishers, and Research Publications, a major micropublisher of records of patents and trademarks, the two for £16.3m,
(c) Warren Gorham Lamont, publishers in the professional fields of law, banking, tax etc for £26.7m,
(d) the publishing interests of Litton Industries, including the Van Nostrand imprint whose chief publishing strengths are in architecture, engineering and electronics, for $63m (subsequently reduced to $40m by disposals),

66

(e) Anaheim Publishing Company bought in 1982, which has given International Thomson the top position as publisher of college mathematical and computer sciences textbooks,

(f) in February 1983 American Banker and The Bond Buyer, both engaged in the financial services industry, at a cost of US$58m.

In the course of little more than four years, Thomsons has acquired and developed information and publishing companies with revenues in excess of US$300m (excluding the American Banker and The Bond Buyer purchases). While the accident of the North Sea clearly makes Thomson's experience very untypical, there are general lessons to be learnt from management's single-minded determination in its pursuit of its chosen goals, and the value it attaches to the position of leadership in a particular sector. Thomsons has the financial strength to bulldoze most competitors out of the way if competition emerges for a particular publisher, while the medium-term character of its objectives enables it to avoid having to show an immediate high pay-back on its purchases. It is now becoming apparent, however, that Thomsons has started to earn some attractive returns following the heavy programme of investment.

Longman's position in the USA as an indigenous publisher dates from 1977 and has so far involved the Group in entering some five different markets both through acquisitions and internal development. This followed the establishment in 1973 of Longman Inc. in New York as a sales outlet for UK published titles. Four years later the decision was taken to start local publishing in medical books and language teaching. In the same year the David McKay college list was acquired from Morgan Grampian. The schools division was set up in New York in 1981 and in 1982 Longman entered the business and professional market with the acquisition of Development Systems Corporation of Chicago; this was followed with the purchase the following year of Caroline House, book distributors based in Aurora, Illinois. In 1983 the Group took the decision to back Longman Crown Inc, a new company aiming to develop educational and training materials for adult learners, and it also purchased Federal Publications Inc. of Washington DC, specialists in the area of construction and contracting and government procurement.

At the end of six years, Longman therefore has a presence in US medical publishing, college publishing, school book publishing, in American language teaching and in business and professional publishing. Geographically, from an initial concentration on New York, Longman now has companies in Illinois and Washington DC. In terms of investment spent, the cumulative total comes to some $22.5m, of which $10m consists of acquisitions (after deducting any cash in the companies acquired) and $12.5m investment in working capital and, to a lesser extent, accumulated losses. The annual rate of sales is running at approximately $28m and the rate of return on sales approaches

10 per cent if one excludes the start-up costs of Longman Crown Inc. (whose own contribution to sales is currently negligible). Large as this investment is in absolute figures, in relation to the American market the sums are far from huge and if the range of sectors across which such investment has been spread is taken into consideration, the amounts invested have in fact been relatively modest. Notwithstanding, there is convincing evidence of profitability. In the next few pages a closer look is given at the various ways management has tackled the task of penetrating widely different US publishing markets.

In medical publishing, which is seen as having considerable potential, Longman is attempting to create a flourishing US operation in a market which it had previously served through exports, often sacrificing the identity of its own imprints in the process. As already noted, since 1977 Longman has been developing its indigenous medical list and at the same time distributing within the USA the titles published in the UK under the Churchill Livingstone imprint. The president and editor in chief, Lewis Reines, is supported by three acquisition editors, whose role has been to develop an American list as well as to build on the strengths of the British list. Initially, it was necessary to promote the imprint vigorously in view of its comparative anonymity in the USA, leading to a heavy direct mail programme, the regular mounting of exhibits and conferences and sizeable journal advertising. Important editorial decisions were also taken, namely to aim at the publication of comprehensive works, whose 'indispensable' character would protect sales should a downturn occur in a market that some believe to be over-supplied with titles. At the same time, the subjects chosen were designed for the most part to meet the needs of affluent specialists rather than of impecunious generalists.

September 1981 witnessed the publication of Churchill Livingstone's first big American book, a two-volume work on Anesthesia; this was the first major US work on the subject, whose American character was immediately evident in the spelling of the title without the usual English diphthong. It was priced 'aggressively' at $98, rather than the $120 price that it might have borne, and sold 15,000 copies in its first year. In terms of profits, it has made a good contribution.

In mid-July 1982, the second major book was published, Operative Hand Surgery priced at $170. This has a useful export potential which Longman's Medical Division based in the UK can be counted on to exploit. While Longman's medical editors in the UK and overseas publish first and foremost for their domestic markets, they benefit from the considerable international marketing strengths of the Group. In the USA this puts them at an advantage over many of their US competitors. One other aspect of Longman's international character arises with the commissioning by UK medical editors of an impressive number of US authors.

At the present time, sales within North America are currently running at around 55 per cent domestic, 45 per cent imports. If, however, Churchill Livingstone Inc.'s own export sales are included in the calculation, its total turnover breaks down into some 70 per cent US originated, 30 per cent imported. The imported titles comprise subjects that are traditionally inter-national in character, such as orthopaedics and haematology, as well as the allied health area, physiotherapy and a small range of student textbooks. The rate of publication of new titles is at around 40 a year, which compares with some 125 for Churchill Livingstone in the UK; the advance in sales of locally published books has been from $600,000 in 1979 to over $4.0m in 1983. Overall sales in 1983, including imported books as well as locally published titles, amounted to some $6m. In terms of distribution, one-half goes to wholesalers for distribution to bookshops, one-quarter is direct mail and one-quarter goes to Longman in the UK for sale there, and in markets serviced from there. In addition, since August 1981, Churchill Livingstone forms part of a group of large medical publishers (Appleton Century Croft, Williams & Wilkins, McGraw-Hill and Churchill Livingstone) and three small firms, whose lists are carried by salesmen to doctors' offices around the country. This adds to the 'visibility' of the imprint and should also provide a use-ful if undramatic additional sales outlet.

Medical publishing in the USA is highly competitive, with perhaps sixty rival imprints and a rapid rate of obsolescence. One aspect of this competitiveness is that Churchill Livingstone has to plan to publish revised editions of its comprehensive works on anesthesia, hand surgery etc every five to six years in order to maintain its position in those sub-jects. Once again, this calls for substantial capital backing.

So far, Longman's experience has been encouraging, with Churchill Livingstone Inc. moving into profit in 1982 and con-solidating this position with a significant improvement in 1983. In terms of market position, Longman can justifiably claim to be already well within the top ten US medical publishers. Were this success to be maintained, Longman's US venture would provide a striking example of how a UK publisher penetrates the USA in an area of specialization, by exploiting the expertise it already possesses and by capitalizing on international strengths that most of its US competitors do not have.

Language teaching is another example of a sector in which Longman is already strongly established outside the USA, with Longman UK in top position as a British exporter. Some time ago, management took the decision to extend its penetration in areas where American English is more appropriate, with the result that 1977 saw the formation in New York of an American English Language Teaching programme. The main markets are the USA, Japan, Canada, Latin America and the Arab world.

69

Separate material has been prepared for secondary and adult age levels. A full course normally comprises six student books, six teachers' guides, six work books, six cassettes and six tapes. The total investment in origination, printing and binding may range between $500,000 and $1,000,000. So far Longman's two development editors have been responsible for two major adult courses, while a course for the secondary level is in preparation. October 1982 saw the recruitment of a third development editor with extensive experience of the USA and Mexican markets.

The marketing of these courses involves direct mail in the United States, as well as through sales representatives. In English-speaking Canada, Longman Inc. is represented by Academic Press (Canada), a subsidiary of Harcourt Brace Jovanovich, and in French Canada, by Didacta in Montreal. In Latin America distributors and licencees are used. Elsewhere in the world, Longman markets the courses, including Japan where Longman has a well-established position.

Competition comes from many of the major US educational publishers including Addison Wesley, Scott Foresman, Harcourt Brace Jovanovich and McGraw-Hill. An aspect of the keen competition is that courses tend to have a limited life with new 'improved' courses being regularly published from one source or another, so that few schools choose to adopt a particular course for more than three years. Consequently, the capital requirements for publishers wishing to sustain a significant position in the market are heavy.

Management's experience since setting out to establish an American Language Teaching presence some six years ago has not surprisingly been that Latin America, the export area having by far the largest potential, has proved harder and more risky than was anticipated. On the other hand, the scope that exists in North America itself has exceeded expectations. To date sales of $3m have been built up and significant expansion is predicted over the next three years; the division must still, however, be regarded as being at a development stage.

In contrast to medical publishing and language teaching, where Longman is grafting on to an existing business a US activity, in college publishing the emphasis is more on developing an independent US operation. The base was provided by the acquisition in 1977 of the David McKay college list, whose main emphasis was in the education market, but where the publishing programme was in urgent need of revival. Education is no longer a glamour area of college publishing: fifteen years ago some 17½ per cent of degrees conferred were in education, now the proportion is less than half at 8 per cent. The silver lining to this cloud is that the major publishers are directing their main efforts at more obvious growth areas such as science and business.

At the same time, Longman is seeking to develop a significant presence in communications, a subject area that is characterized by growth but where the scale is more appropriate to Longman's North American style of publishing than it is to the major US educational houses. Courses in communications are given in the third and fourth years of undergraduate study and that means that the big introductory text is not appropriate.

Many of the books involved may have sales of 2,000 to 5,000 copies a year. This is of marginal interest to the big units in educational publishing who have vast sales forces (175 college representatives for Prentice Hall) to keep occupied, and heavy overheads. A firm of Longman's type can, however, make such publishing pay, particularly if use is made of its experience in print buying. The composition costs on low-run titles of this kind can account for half the production costs and if composition is done in the Far East it may be at half the price that would have been charged in America; this represents a saving of one-quarter in total production costs.

The other aspect of educational publishing that Longman has entered is the vast Elhi market (elementary and high school market). The approach is, however, highly selective, aimed at publishing in areas and numbers that are unattractive to the US giants in the industry. There is no question at this stage of direct confrontation in respect, say, of the adoption of standard texts in high school courses in the major subjects, which can sell in hundreds of thousands of copies.

At the high school (and junior college) level, Longman's interests include history, where the emphasis is on the Ancient World up to the Middle Ages, using material produced in the UK, and on the twentieth century, where the main text is supported by a wide range of ancillary publications of a kind that are not produced in the USA. Finally, an example of a subject that is largely ignored by US publishers is Latin where Longman currently has approximately 5 per cent of the US market, with Cambridge University Press providing its main competition. A recent conspicuous success has been the adoption of Longman's Latin course in the State of Texas. For a foreign publisher, this is a signal achievement, given the somewhat chauvinistic reactions that are sometimes met when selling to public sector schools. Conversely, Longman does benefit from a certain cachet as a UK publisher when selling to private schools.

In Elhi publishing, Longman's approach is characterized by considerable caution. So far, the local publishing content has been limited largely to adapting to US standards books already published for the UK schools market. It has been a question of exploiting more fully existing UK material by taking advantage of Longman's physical presence in the US market. Longman's Elhi involvement is still at an early stage of development.

Perhaps the greatest potential for growth is seen as being in professional and business publishing. In this area, there is no question of building on to an existing strength within Longman's activities, hence the important role played by acquisitions in the development so far.

The first step was the acquisition, in March 1982, of Development Systems Corporation of Chicago, whose net tangible assets amounted to $550,000. Robert Kyle had founded DSC some fifteen years previously; a condition of the purchase was that he should remain totally involved in the business. Under the imprint, Real Estate Education Company, DSC occupies the leading position as publisher of texts, professional books and other materials for teaching real estate practice and law. Its basic text, Modern Real Estate Practice, is used in more than 1,500 colleges and universities and private real estate business schools. In the past few years, DSC has also been developing material for the practising real estate professional and for allied professionals requiring real estate material in such fields as insurance, property management, banking, accountancy and law. The next stage of expansion is likely to take the company more deeply into the financial services area, including banking, insurance and the securities industry. In 1983 sales were in excess of $3m.

From the start of September 1983, Longman has given its backing to a new enterprise, Longman Crown Inc., whose goal is to produce and market educational and training materials for adult learners, with an initial emphasis on the area of computer technology. Its target consists of workers in business and industry who require training and retraining. The material produced will combine print and microcomputer software for home study use as well as for use at work and in the classroom. In this instance, Longman is backing a small team of four highly qualified individuals who are already experienced in this area; they have been given the assurance of access to substantial funds, subject to their meeting certain targets, which will provide them with the opportunity of creating specialist training packages, part of whose originality lies in linking home, work place and classroom study.

A further important development in Longman's US expansion in business and professional publishing came with the acquisition, in October 1983, of Federal Publications Inc. of Washington DC at a cost of $8.5m (including the cash in the balance sheet). The company specializes in publications (chiefly journals and newsletters) and seminars on construction, contracting and US Government procurement, and has as its main audience businessmen and attorneys. It was started some years ago by the present proprietor, Henry Kaiser, and has been built up to a business with sales of $7m. Longman lays particular stress on the value of the strong links it is gaining in Washington DC which are seen as a key requirement in information publishing in the USA. It foresees further useful growth under the existing management which could come about in part through purchases of compatible businesses.

In considering Longman's entry into US business and professional publishing an ingredient that is common to all developments so far has been the fact that Longman has been backing management. In as much as Longman is entering a field that is new to it, this is perhaps hardly surprising. What is interesting is that Longman's style of business is attracting to it successful entrepreneurs who, while realizing some of their investment, remain ambitious for the further development of their businesses. One of these, Robert Kyle, head of Development Systems Corporation, has moreover been appointed president of Longman's newly created US holding company to which all the US interests barring the medical division now report. The creation of 'an environment that is entrepreneurial but not too entrepreneurial' to quote Longman's deputy chief executive, Michael Wyman, coupled with availability of substantial capital resources can clearly act as a powerful magnet to privately owned businesses.

Comment

In considering the illustrations given above of UK companies' differing approaches to the US market, a few general points come to mind. First of all, it is by no means appropriate for all UK firms to have a direct presence in the US market. This is not just a question of size (though obviously many are ruled out by that consideration alone) but also of publishing profile. To take an extreme example, Octopus's substantial US sales are achieved through skilful marketing arrangements and with no direct presence.

In trade publishing, British firms have for the most part adopted the 'slow but steady' approach 'progressing' from:
(a) the sale of US rights through
(b) a distribution arrangement in the USA;
(c) an office of their own in the USA with a sales monitoring function;
(d) the assumption of a more direct sales role involving an increasing number of their own representatives;
(e) the development of a local list, with the recruiting of one or more US editors.

In more specialist publishing, one approach has been to identify areas where the UK publisher has a strength and which are of little attraction currently to the US firms; this involves going for the crumbs from the table and minimizing direct conflict with the US majors. Associated Book Publishers' postgraduate geography list and Longman's tactics in Elhi and college publishing are instances of this.

Another approach is to take the battle directly to the enemy's lines, as with Longman's American Language Teaching and medical lists. In both cases, it involves the company in maximizing such advantages as it has over the US firms through its considerable international exposure. Viking Penguin also aims to exploit as effectively as possible the international strengths of the Penguin Group.

In the more specialist areas of publishing, the capital requirements can well be heavy, particularly where a significant presence is aimed at. This has led in the past - and is likely to continue to do so in the future - to acquisitions. The experience of UK publishers in this area has been mixed. The happiest and most convincing experience has so far been that of International Thomson, whose financial strength has enabled them to acquire, from the outset, management as well as publishing assets. The evidence from Longman is also encouraging, though that company is less advanced in the development of its American publishing interests than is International Thomson. The experience of the two groups does in addition suggest as a tentative comment that UK companies can offer an attractive home to successful US publishers who want an environment that permits the preservation of the separate identity of their firms and at the same time offers scope for further expansion. A velvet glove that is rarely worn by the larger US firms.

AUSTRALIA

1. Australian Population Trends

The projections in Table 46 indicate an annual rate of population growth in the 1981 to 1991 decade of 1.5 per cent, which is identical to that for the 1971 to 1981 decade. This maintained rate of increase in turn means a significant expansion in absolute numbers.

Table 46

Australian Population Trends

(thousands)	1971	1976	1981	1986	1991	1996
TOTAL	12,761	13,916	14,846	15,983	17,255	18,582
0-19	4,792	5,015	4,997	5,097	5,310	5,593
0-4	1,212	1,232	1,138	1,250	1,419	1,482
5-9	1,223	1,276	1,267	1,193	1,305	1,479
10-14	1,245	1,258	1,306	1,310	1,237	1,352
15-19	1,112	1,249	1,286	1,344	1,349	1,280
20-64	6,889	7,665	8,304	9,228	10,019	10,823
20-34	2,791	3,307	3,700	3,939	4,200	4,329
35-44	1,518	1,580	1,835	2,240	2,529	2,727
45-64	2,580	2,778	2,769	3,049	3,290	3,767
65+	1,080	1,236	1,545	1,657	1,925	2,166

Sources: Australian Year Books, 1972 and 1975/7; Projections of the Population of Australia, 1981 to 2002, Australian Bureau of Statistics, August 1981

The age-group breakdown presented in Table 47 shows a continuation of little growth in the 0-19 age brackets, while such growth that is anticipated among the 0-19-year-olds is furthermore weighted towards the youngest age brackets. The main area of expansion is consequently concentrated in the broad 20-64 age band where the numbers are quite significant, and where growth is fairly evenly divided between the three bands chosen: the 20-34-year-olds, who may be said to make up the family formation bracket, the 35-44-year-olds, who bear the brunt of educational and leisure outlays on children, and the 45-64-year-olds, who are shedding their family responsibilities and turning towards the challenges of retirement.

Table 47

Australian Population Changes 1971 to 1991

(thousands)	1971 to 1976	1976 to 1981	(1971 to 1981)	1981 to 1986	1986 to 1991	(1981 to 1991)
TOTAL	+1,155	+930	+2,085	+1,137	+1,272	+2,409
0-19	+223	-18	+205	+100	+213	+313
0-4	+20	-94	-74	+112	+169	+281
5-9	+53	-9	+44	-74	+112	+38
10-14	+13	+48	+61	+4	-73	-69
15-19	+137	+37	+174	+58	+5	+63
20-64	+776	+639	+1,415	+924	+791	+1,715
20-34	+516	+393	+909	+239	+261	+500
35-44	+62	+255	+317	+405	+289	+694
45-64	+198	-9	+189	+280	+241	+521
65+	+156	+309	+465	+112	+268	+380

Source: Derived from Table 46

From the point of view of UK publishers, the first observation is that Australia is one of the traditional markets where population changes are, _ceteris paribus_, going to be a source of buoyancy throughout the current decade. In terms of the population pyramid, the numbers are not, however, going to be particularly helpful to strictly educational publishers. Instead, it is those publishers who satisfy the leisure and instructional needs of the working population who will be benefiting most from the impetus that sizeable population expansion may be expected to provide.

2. The Australian Book Market

The Australian book trade consists of some 200 firms, though if all organizations who publish books in any one year are taken into account, the total comes to approximately 260. Australian book publishing is made up of large numbers of comparatively small firms: out of the total of 200, only about 20 per cent have sales in excess of A$2m, while the majority are below A$1m. The largest publisher/distributor - William Collins - had a turnover in 1982 believed to have been around A$40m. Among other sizeable groups, three are Australian owned - Rigby Publishers, Landsdowne Press and Angus & Robertson/Bay Books.

Table 48 summarizes some salient statistics relating to the Australian book market covering the four years for which information is available.

Table 48

Selected Australian Book Publishing Statistics

Year to December 31	1979	1980	1981	1982
(A$million)				
Estimated retail book sales*	450	502	551	590
Book imports+	160	163	182	202
Book exports	NA	17	19	19
Estimated publishers' sales* in Australia	258	288	317	339
of which,				
Australian books	NA	41.6%	46.3%	50.8%
Imported books	NA	58.4%	53.7%	49.2%
New Australian titles published	2,412	2,656	2,171	2,443
No. of publishers in Australia	258	261	262	263

* Total net receipts to publishers (excluding exports) grossed up for incomplete coverage (80 per cent coverage estimated) gives estimated book publishers' sales. Grossed up in turn for 42.5 per cent average bookseller discount gives estimated retail book sales. + To 30 June of following year
Sources: Australian Book Publishers Association, The Australian Bookseller

One general point to make on the subject of Australian book publishing statistics is that, while there is a sustained and encouraging drive to improve their quality, considerable caution must be exercised in the use of historical series. All too frequently one year is not comparable with another.

The estimates of total retail book sales in Table 48 exclude throughout export sales. Were they to have been included in 1982 this would have given a total of A$630m. Over the four years covered in the table, retail sales in Australian books (excluding exports) are shown as having risen by 31 per cent in value terms. Over the same period, the consumer price index rose by 34 per cent, suggesting no real growth at all. Based on the way these necessarily rough and ready estimates are constructed, the same conclusion applies to estimated publishers' sales in Australia.

The somewhat slower growth of imports discussed in greater detail later is linked to the decline in the relative importance of foreign books from 58.4 per cent of publishers' sales in 1980, to 49.2 per cent in 1982, and the commensurate increase in the share of Australian books, which went from 41.6 per cent to 50.8 per cent. Given a swing of this magnitude, while the overall book market may have shown little growth in real terms, considerable opportunities will have existed for firms engaged in local publishing. It is of symbolic significance as well, that Australian books should have nosed ahead of imported books for the first time. The ABPA warns, however, that the firms reporting from one year to another (119 in 1982) are not necessarily the same and that in 1982 Encyclopaedia Britannica, Field Educational Enterprises and Grolier ceased to be members of the Association and stopped supplying figures; the three are typically sizeable importers. Another aspect of Australian publishing that is studied in some detail is the nationality of ownership within the industry.

Table 49

Australian Book Publishing Market Share by Nationality of Ownership

(per cent)	1980 Educ	Gen	Total*	1981 Educ	Gen	Total*	1982 Educ	Gen	Total*
UK	29	43	37	33	40	37	45	41	42
USA	57	30	41	48	28	35	31	28	29
Australia	14	21	18	19	32	27	24	30	28
Other	–	6	4	–	1	1	–	1	1
	100	100	100	100	100	100	100	100	100

* Including rights income, of which some 70 per cent accrues to Australian publishers and 25 per cent to UK publishers. Exports are also included.
Source: Australian Book Publishers Association

Table 49 presents the figures for three years. Once again the caveat has to be made that a changing mix of firms reporting each year may distort the year-to-year comparisons. In particular, the omissions noted earlier for 1982 will have artificially depressed the US figures. Nonetheless the general pattern probably remains valid, with UK companies maintaining their share of the overall market, Australian companies substantially increasing theirs, amd US firms losing market share.

Since 1978, the ABPA has presented a statistically consistent series covering 18 of the larger firms in the industry, which form a sample or Control Group. With total revenues in 1982 of A$112m, they accounted for some 31 per cent of the industry-wide revenues and consequently provide a useful insight into trends in Australian publishing.

Table 50

ABPA Analysis of Returns by 18 Member Firms of Control Group - Sales

(A$millions/per cent)	1978		1979		1980		1981		1982	
Education	35.5	100	39.1	100	43.4	100	49.5	100	51.6	100
of which										
Australian bks	16.7	46.9	18.9	48.2	21.5	49.6	25.7	51.9	29.0	56.2
Imported books	18.8	53.1	20.2	51.8	21.9	50.4	23.8	48.1	22.6	43.8
General	38.9	100	43.0	100	41.2	100	43.1	100	56.4	100
of which										
Australian bks	10.9	28.1	13.2	30.6	12.0	29.1	11.8	27.3	14.7	26.1
Imported books	28.0	71.9	29.9	69.4	29.2	70.9	31.3	72.7	41.7	73.9
Total sales in Australia	74.4	100	82.2	100	84.6	100	92.6	100	108.1	100
of which										
Australian bks	27.6	37.1	32.0	39.0	33.5	39.6	37.4	40.4	43.7	40.5
Imported books	46.8	62.9	50.2	61.0	51.1	60.4	55.2	59.6	64.3	59.5
Exports	3.0		3.2		3.1		3.0		3.4	
TOTAL SALES	77.4		85.4		87.7		95.6		111.5	

Note: The first analysis of this kind dates from 1978, since when the eighteen member firms of the Control Group have supplied annual returns to a fixed questionnaire. Where discrepancies exist, this is due to rounding.
Source: Australian Book Publishers Association

Table 49 also adds detail to the overall trend discussed above of sales growth being concentrated on Australian books as distinct from imported books. In the educational sector, the local publisher now dominates the market following a sales increase for the Control Group companies over the period 1978-82 of 74 per cent compared to a rise of 20 per cent for imported educational books. Adjusting for inflation of 47 per cent, local educational publishing has experienced real growth while imports have failed to match price increases.

Table 51

ABPA Analysis of Returns by 55 Member Firms

Turnover	1980		1981		1982	
(A$thousands/per cent)						
Education	61,201	100	70,883	100	76,897	100
of which						
Australian books	28,445	46.5	35,377	49.9	41,690	54.2
Imported books	32,756	53.5	35,506	50.1	35,207	45.8
General	96,525	100	115,465	100	132,271	100
of which						
Australian books	41,799	43.3	52,754	45.7	60,280	45.6
Imported books	54,726	56.7	62,711	54.3	71,991	54.4
Sale of rights in Australia	171		249		152	
Total sales in Australia	157,897	100	186,597	100	209,320	100
of which						
Australian books	70,244	44.5	88,131	47.2	101,970	48.7
Imported books	87,482	55.4	98,217	52.6	107,198	51.2
Sale of rights in Australia	171	0.1	249	0.2	152	0.1
Exports	12,023		15,738		15,622	
TOTAL TURNOVER	169,920		202,335		224,942	

Note: Where minor discrepancies exist, this is due to rounding.
Source: Australian Book Publishers Association

In general books, the experience of the Control Group sample does not suggest any marked trend: imported books would still appear to dominate the market, and indeed the percentage of general book sales accounted for by imports rose slightly from 71.9 per cent in 1978 to 73.9 per cent in 1982. Over the period sales growth of imports came to 49 per cent, and of Australian books to 35 per cent, which compares with an increase in the consumer price index of 47 per cent.

Exports have been on a rising trend - but still only accounted for 3 per cent of the total revenues in 1982.

Another set of statistics is now available from the Australian Book Publishers Association. It is, in effect, an expanded control group covering consistent returns from fifty-five companies, which together account for some 63 per cent of industry sales. The period covered is three years. The information is set out in Table 51 in the same form as Table 50.

A comparison with Table 50 confirms the changing pattern of educational sales, though the percentage share of Australian books is slightly lower, and, of imported books, correspondingly higher. The main contrast lies in general books, where the enlarged sample in Table 51 gives Australian books a much more respectable percentage at 45.6 per cent in 1982, compared to 26.1 per cent in the smaller sample.

Over the three years covered in the table, total revenues advanced by 32 per cent; this compares to a rise in the consumer price index of 22 per cent, indicating a measure of real growth which stands in encouraging contrast to the static picture that the longer historical series provides. Educational book sales rose 26 per cent (47 per cent for Australian books and only 7 per cent for imports), while general book sales showed growth well in excess of price rises at 37 per cent (44 per cent for Australian books and 32 per cent for imported books).

Hardbacks/Paperbacks

Reverting to Table 48, retail book sales of A$590m in 1982 may have been made up of approximately 80 per cent hardbacks, 15 per cent mass-market paperbacks and 5 per cent other paperbacks. The detailed paperback statistics in Table 52 relate to seven mass-market paperback firms and are believed to account for some 85 per cent of paperback sales in Australia.

Deducting net mass-market paperback sales at retail value from total Australian retail book sales it emerges that the rate of growth of paperbacks from 1979 to 1982 has been somewhat faster at 39 per cent than has been the case of hardbacks and non-mass-market paperbacks at 30 per cent. In volume terms, the minimal rise in children's paperbacks since 1978 and the actual decline in adult paperbacks comes as somewhat of a

81

surprise. The figures shown are after adjusting for incomplete coverage where information on units sold has not been supplied and the ABPA Paperback Committee warns that caution should be used in utilizing these unit statistics. One of the more striking developments was the severe deterioration in the rate of returns to nearly 36 per cent in 1980; that year witnessed the collapse of two important trade distributors, Rical and Novalit. In 1981, the situation became much healthier, only for there to be a relapse in the recessionary year of 1982.

Table 52

Australian Mass-market Paperback Statistics

	1978	1979	1980	1981	1982
(A$thousands)					
Gross retail sales	69,400*	86,020*	97,620	102,582	128,354
Rate of returns (%)	22.0	25.8	35.8	23.6	30.4
Net retail sales,	54,100	63,852	62,704	78,370	89,347
of which					
adult	49,736	58,747	57,230	70,942	81,064
children's	4,364	5,105	5,474	7,429	8,283
(units)					
Retail sales,	20,250	20,100	17,550	19,450	19,650
of which					
adult	17,750	17,750	15,150	16,900	17,100
children's	2,500	2,350	2,400	2,550	2,550

*Excluding Sphere
Notes: The figures represent an estimated 85 per cent of total paperback sales in Australia. Where minor discrepancies exist, this is due to rounding.
Source: Australian Book Publishers Association

Imports

The Australian import statistics, shown in Table 53 reveal an annual rate of growth of imports by value over the full six years of 11.5 per cent with imports of paperbacks advancing slightly less rapidly than those of hardbacks.

Table 53

Australian Book Imports

To June 30	1976-77	1977-78	1978-79	1979-80	1980-81	1981-82	1982-83
(A$million)							
TOTAL, of which	105.0	112.4	148.3	160.2	163.4	181.8	201.8
UK	44.6	53.9	71.1	74.4	73.4	73.0	81.0
USA	42.2	37.6	43.7	48.9	52.5	65.5	74.0
Asia	18.2	20.9	22.3	23.2	26.3	31.2	33.3
Other	NA	NA	11.2	13.7	11.2	12.1	13.5
Paperbacks							
TOTAL, of which	41.1	47.5	58.2	64.3	65.2	68.7	77.1
UK	22.9	28.0	36.9	33.9	34.9	33.2	34.9
USA	13.7	13.0	14.4	16.5	17.7	21.7	27.0
Asia	4.5	6.5	6.9	8.3	8.0	8.9	9.7
Other	NA	NA	NA	5.6	4.6	4.9	5.5
Hardbacks							
TOTAL, of which	63.9	64.9	78.9	95.9	98.2	113.1	124.7
UK	21.7	25.9	34.2	40.5	38.5	39.8	46.1
USA	28.5	24.6	29.3	32.4	34.8	43.8	47.0
Asia	13.7	14.4	15.4	14.9	18.3	22.3	23.6
Other	NA	NA	NA	8.1	6.6	7.2	8.0

Annual Rates of Change

(per cent)	1976-77 to 1982-83	1979-80 to 1982-83
TOTAL, of which	+11.5	+8.0
UK	+10.3	+2.9
USA	+9.8	+14.8
Asia	+10.6	+12.8
Other	NA	-0.5
Paperbacks		
TOTAL, of which	+11.0	+6.3
UK	+7.3	+1.0
USA	+12.0	+17.8
Asia	+13.6	+5.3
Other	NA	-0.6
Hardbacks		
TOTAL, of which	+11.8	+9.1
UK	+13.4	+4.4
USA	+8.7	+13.2
Asia	+9.5	+16.6
Other	NA	-0.4

Source: Australian Bureau of Statistics, Australian Book Publishers Association

Over the full six-year period, imports from the UK maintained a comparatively high rate of growth. In the latest three-year period, however, such imports slowed markedly and this was accompanied by a rapid expansion in Australian purchases from the USA. Imports from Asia represent to a large extent books that Australian publishers have had manufactured in Hong Kong, Japan and Singapore. In 1982, for instance, the eighteen firms forming the Control Group bought 57 per cent of their print requirements in Asia and only 38 per cent in Australia.

An alternative source of information on imports from the USA is the US Commerce Department, one aspect of which is that the figures are available for an extended period of time. US book exports to Australia are broken down into seven categories in Table 54 which covers an eleven-year span.

Table 54

US Book Exports to Australia

(US$million)	1972	1973	1974	1975	1976	1977	1978
TOTAL, of which	13.82	17.44	23.40	27.93	29.59	27.90	36.71
Bibles	0.67	0.75	1.20	1.07	1.36	1.53	2.24
Dictionaries	0.31	0.31	0.73	0.59	0.53	1.40	0.48
Encyclopaedias	3.15	3.18	5.03	5.16	6.10	4.43	4.14
Textbooks	1.93	2.05	3.99	4.36	4.40	3.94	5.17
Technical books	2.23	4.38	2.52	6.24	5.61	5.61	6.65
Other	4.31	5.33	7.95	8.87	10.71	10.65	16.04
Picture books	1.22	1.44	1.98	1.64	0.88	0.35	2.00

(US$million)	1979	1980	1981	1982	Nine months 1982	1983
TOTAL, of which	40.69	39.03	53.36	57.02	44.59	39.89
Bibles	2.28	2.43	2.66	3.75	2.74	2.47
Dictionaries	0.65	0.33	0.75	0.86	0.86	0.13
Encyclopaedias	5.17	5.00	4.85	5.57	5.07	7.38
Textbooks	5.43	4.40	7.72	7.43	5.84	4.16
Technical books	5.86	4.47	5.90	8.53	6.31	6.37
Other	19.20	19.78	27.68	28.17	21.74	17.31
Picture books	2.10	2.62	3.80	2.71	2.03	2.07

Note: Where minor discrepancies exist, this is due to rounding
Source: US Department of Commerce

Throughout the ten years, total US exports to Australia in value terms maintained a remarkably consistent annual rate of growth at around 15 per cent. The fastest expansion was achieved by bibles and by the residual 'other' category. Looking at the five-year periods, the main feature was a slowing down in the import of technical books, which have furthermore shown a fair degree of volatility from one year to another. The vagaries of the rates of change of imports of dictionaries and picture books reflect exceptional figures in 1977. For consistent growth at a high rate textbooks and bibles are the prime examples.

Table 55

Rates of Change in US Book Exports to Australia

(per cent)	1972-1977	1977-1982	1972-1982
TOTAL, of which	+15.1	+15.4	+15.2
Bibles	+18.0	+19.6	+18.8
Dictionaries	+36.4	-9.3	+10.7
Encyclopaedias	+7.1	+4.7	+5.8
Textbooks	+15.4	+13.5	+14.4
Technical books	+20.3	+8.7	+14.4
Other	+20.0	+21.5	+20.6
Picture books	-22.1	+50.6	+8.3

Source: Derived from US Department of Commerce

If one considers the very recent past, one of the most striking developments is the way in which US imports continued to expand in Australian dollar terms through to June 1983. Expressed in US dollars, growth was sustained throughout calendar 1982 and it was only in the first nine months of 1983 that a 10½ per cent drop was recorded. In the face of a strong US dollar - which, moreover, has been contributing to a severe deterioration in the overall US current account balance - this performance can be explained by:
(a) the long lead times in the promotion and ordering of books which make it difficult to link fluctuations in exchange rates to the import statistics,
(b) the dominant position enjoyed by certain US publishers, notably in the tertiary educational field, which makes US books indispensable purchases at more or less any price,
(c) the impact of the rise of the dollar on value figures, which can disguise a much less dynamic experience in unit terms.
While the truth no doubt incorporates an element of all three influences, the price inelastic characteristic of demand for many US book imports is undoubtedly impressive.

3. Australian Publishing

Australian publishers' output in terms of titles (Table 56) shows a gradual but erratic upward trend in the period 1974-82. This contrasts with the pattern of yearly increases that has been typical of the UK and the USA.

Table 56

Australian Publishers' Output by Title

| | January-June | | July-December | | January-December | |
	No. of titles	Average price (A$)	No. of titles	Average price (A$)	No. of titles	Average price (A$)
1983	755	11.94				
1982	764	10.41	1,679	11.33	2,443	11.04
1981	852	10.34	1,318	10.93	2,171	10.70
1980	752	9.68	1,904	10.47	2,656	10.24
1979	686	11.75	1,726	9.77	2,412	10.33
1978	770	7.16	1,413	8.03	2,183	7.73
1977	663	7.30	1,580	7.39	2,243	7.37
1976	529	6.04	1,252	6.91	1,781	6.65
1975	719	5.19	1,282	6.31	2,001	5.91
1974	607	NA	1,008	NA	1,615	NA

Source: Australian Bookseller and Publisher

In Table 57, publishers have been classified under four headings - 'Selected UK Houses', 'Selected US Houses', 'Selected Australian Houses' and 'Balance - Primarily Australian'.

As is made clear by the table, the publishing activity of individual firms in terms of titles can vary widely from one year to the next. Also, it must be accepted that the number of titles published is an extremely crude measure of such activity. Nonetheless, it is of interest to note certain contrasts that emerge between groups. The most striking of these is the way in which UK firms have increased their share of titles published from an average of 18.0 per cent in 1975-76 to an average of 25.3 per cent in 1981-82, a considerable advance by any standards. At the same time US publishers have seen their share of titles published stay little changed: 7.4 per cent in 1975-76 and 7.8 per cent in 1981-82, the advance being entirely attributed to Jacaranda. Taken at its face value, UK firms have responded vigorously to the familiar Australian plea of more local publishing and less dependence on imports in a way that US publishers have either chosen not to or been unable to do.

It should be noted that the ABPA has published tables for the three years 1980-82 showing new titles published, broken down by nationality of ownership. The totals differ from those presented in Table 57: for 1982, the UK proportion is 30.9 per cent, the US 10.4 per cent, the Australian 57.1 per cent and there is a residual figure of 1.6 per cent. The present table's main merit may be judged to lie in the fact that it extends over a longer period of time and that individual publishing firms are identified. It would appear, however, that there is a significant understatement of the UK and, to a much lesser extent, of the US figures.

If one ignores the figures for the first half of 1983, which could prove unrepresentative since first half titles normally account for less than 30 per cent of the total for the year, the analysis of titles published by Australian houses shows the large groups broadly holding their own, while the residual grouping has seen its share decline gradually. The evidence of the increasing role of large firms, whether Australian or foreign-backed, does not, however, change significantly the industry's characteristic of considerable fragmentation.

4. Indigenous Publishing and Local Selling

The statistics shown have already highlighted the development of Australian educational publishing, whose growth has far outstripped that of imported educational titles. The statistical evidence relates to a recent period, but is part of a very much longer process. It was in 1962, for example, that the first Australian Book Week was held, demonstrating after a fashion the coming of age of the Australian publishing trade.

In the publication of general books (ie non-educational) various attempts have been made to calculate changes in the relative importance of Australian publishing. It has been estimated that in 1972 Australian books sold accounted for 10 per cent of the total, and imports for 90 per cent. In 1980 the proportions were 41 per cent and 59 per cent and for 1982, a 50/50 split may not be too wide of the mark. Another way of looking at the subject is through the eyes of the retail trade. Collins Book Depot in Melbourne, for example, estimates that 40 per cent of its business is now in Australian titles and 60 per cent in imported books. Some twenty-five years ago, the proportions would have been closer to 10 per cent Australian and 90 per cent imported.

Another way of considering the evolution of indigenous publishing is to look briefly at the experience of a number of foreign publishing houses.

Table 57 - New Titles Published by Selected Publishers

	1975	1976	1977	1978	1979	1980	1981	1982	1983*
Selected UK houses									
Allen & Unwin	-	-	4	16	20	20	31	37	16
ABP Law Books	23	22	13	23	37	16	18	19	2
ABP Methuen	10	6	13	16	44	45	42	59	6
Edward Arnold	7	8	8	21	12	5	5	11	-
Butterworth	34	20	10	21	1	27	23	23	15
Collins	25	24	23	45	44	26	27	42	28
CUP	20	20	11	3	-	9	9	5	-
Heinemann (ex.H-Ginn)	18	17	19	29	16	10	28	16	4
Hodder	12	15	17	9	21	20	12	19	-
Hutchinson	10	8	4	24	-	12	15	21	2
Longman Cheshire	30	10	28	38	31	59	54	72	12
Macmillan	65	21	83	28	98	72	78	21	7
Sun	18	18	31	35	29	20	16	10	5
Nelson	38	62	58	61	72	114	102	94	20
OUP	7	8	7	21	28	40	36	33	1
Pan	-	-	-	-	-	3	11	9	-
Penguin	30	27	19	29	18	41	55	47	15
Pergamon	9	11	15	9	9	6	9	11	5
Pitman	13	17	5	47	26	32	12	30	23
Subtotal	369	314	369	475	506	577	583	579	161
As % of total	18.4	17.6	16.5	21.8	21.0	21.7	26.9	23.7	21.3
Selected US houses									
Addison-Wesley	-	-	33	-	18	6	-	2	3
Cassells	41	38	5	48	24	37	7	8	-
CCH	-	-	14	4	16	35	42	33	21
Doubleday	-	-	-	9	3	4	14	13	8

Harcourt	–	14	6	30	32	18	6	3	5
Holt Saunders	12	2	3	2	12	19	27	22	25
McGraw Hill	–	8	14	30	21	12	30	34	65
Van Nostrand	–	–	3	4	3	9	9	1	3
Wiley	–	–	–	–	–	–	2	22	23
Jacaranda	14	102	52	50	67	27	29		
Subtotal	58	222	141	198	196	146	155	120	162
As % of total	7.7	9.1	6.5	7.5	8.1	6.7	6.9	6.7	8.1
Selected Australian houses									
Angus & Robertson	40	110	112	154	136	117	177	144	152
Bay Books	1	28	26	37	38	42	10	–	–
Horwitz Group	56	209	192	211	173	204	192	134	130
Lansdowne	16	53	44	53	19	11	13	20	18
Rigby	42	134	52	191	128	258	268	134	148
Subtotal	155	534	426	646	494	632	660	432	448
As % of total	20.5	21.9	19.6	24.3	20.5	29.0	29.4	24.3	22.4
Balance – Overwhelmingly Australian									
Subtotal	381	1,108	1,021	1,235	1,216	930	1,059	915	1,022
As % of total	50.5	45.4	47.0	46.5	50.4	42.6	47.2	51.4	51.1
TOTAL	755	2,443	2,171	2,656	2,412	2,183	2,243	1,781	2,001

* First half year only.   Source: <u>Australian Bookseller and Publisher</u>

Longman undertook its first local publishing in the 1950s. The real thrust dates, however, from the late 1960s, and in 1976 a quantum jump was made with the acquisition from Xerox Corporation of the Australian Cheshire Group, which was some three times the size of Longman Australia and very much more deeply entrenched than Longman. This has been supplemented by the much smaller Reed Educational and Sorrett acquisitions in 1979 and 1981. In September 1983 Longman Cheshire purchased from Addison-Wesley a further Primary Reading Programme; this should add some A$500,000 to Group turnover.

The Longman Cheshire Group's current turnover of some A$11½m is made up of four-fifths indigenous publishing and one-fifth imports, the latter comprising such series as the Breakthrough to Literacy. The Australian publishing is supported by four and a half commissioning editors. Some 20 per cent of the Group's sales are at present at the primary level, 70 per cent secondary and 10 per cent tertiary; in terms of market share, the company estimates that it now has 8 per cent of the primary market and 14 per cent of the secondary market. Local titles in print number 1,250.

Part of Longman Australia's strategy has clearly been to use the 'muscle' that its position within the Pearson Group has given it to develop organically and through acquisition to the point where economies of scale are achieved. Typically, the purchases have been financed through local borrowings. Another feature of Longman's operations is the sub-contracting of the warehousing and distribution to its sister company, Penguin. Longman Cheshire for its part has two sales executives for the tertiary titles (one for the medical list and one for the non-medical list) and about ten representatives for primary and secondary selling; Longman Cheshire also handles the mailing programmes, which are heavy, at all three educational levels. The financial targets of the Group are a return on sales of 15 per cent, and on capital employed of 40 per cent. The objectives over the next few years continue to lie in the extension of market share, leading to further economies of scale. With little assistance from population growth in the decade to 1991 (which follows a flat decade in the educational age bracket between 1971 and 1981) the market is bound to continue to be competitive. At the primary and secondary levels, however, competition from US publishers seems likely to remain less of a threat.

Heinemann Australia is an example of a firm that has not aspired to achieve the scale of Longman's operations, but has succeeded in building a secure position in secondary educational publishing, very largely based on indigenous publishing. In 1983, 50 per cent of total sales amounting to approximately A$4¼m were from the Australian list and 50 per cent represented imports (including the agency for Hutchinson Educational); 73 per cent of total sales were educational and 27 per cent trade.

The educational side has as its foundation Heinemann's _Australian Dictionary for Schools_, the first of its kind when it was published in 1976. For a firm of Heinemann Australia's size, a project of this kind represented a major financial gamble. One measure of the investment called for is the fact that it meant the use of four lexicographers working full time for four years in the period 1972-76. The continuing success of the Heinemann title - despite the fact that there are now five locally produced Australian dictionaries - gives Heinemann Australia a valuable flow of back-list income. With the dictionary on computer storage, spin-offs are being developed. The financial security it provides is also enabling Heinemann Australia to publish other educational titles, which reflect management's view that the days of the monolithic prescribed textbook are past and that greater scope lies in books that have narrower targets.

In addition, the strength of the position in educational publishing is helping to sustain Heinemann Australia's programme of developing its general list based on local publishing. In the light of the largely static school-age population over the next few years, as well as the possibility that government funding for education will remain tight for some time, a more balanced educational/general publishing pattern of business would seem to be desirable.

Collins is a major force in the Australian book scene both in terms of distribution - where it shares with Gordon & Gotch the distinction of providing a nationwide service - and in local non-educational publishing. Collins' distribution side was built up in the 1970s, firstly with the acquisition in 1972 of Forlib (renamed Collins Forlib) which distributed in Victoria, Western Australia and South Australia, and then, in 1974, with the purchase of Leutenegger, whose business was in Queensland and New South Wales. In 1978 a major new distribution centre was opened at Moss Vale (some 150 kilometres outside Sydney) which replaced four existing warehouses; the warehouse not affected was the one at Perth. In sterling terms the total cost came to £2.25m. The scale of the operation is indicated by the fact that the distribution side currently employs about 300 people, of whom roughly one-third is involved with sales, one-third with the handling of the books and one-third in marketing and all aspects of administration. The sales team includes 50 responsible for the mass-market, 15 selling trade paperbacks to traditional bookshops, 15 selling hardbacks to traditional outlets, and a numerically small team dealing with special sales, direct mail and so forth. These sales forces are organized geographically with a sales office in all state capitals, barring Hobart. Collins distribution naturally takes in its own titles whether originated in the UK or in Australia, and includes Fontana. In addition Collins distributes and warehouses for a number of other publishers.

In indigenous publishing, there are three aspects to Collins's activities:
(i)   a children's list with 10-12 new titles a year, which makes Collins the largest publisher in this sector;
(ii)   a hardback list featuring quality fiction and literature - ie the <u>Collins Book of Australian Poetry</u> - and Australian natural history, with an annual rate of 10-12 new titles;
(iii) Fontana's list of books on Australian subjects, involving two to three publications a month.

Taken together, this gives Collins a powerful position in Australian publishing, an area of further planned growth. One relatively recent example was the formation in mid-1982 of Collins Liturgical Australia; this follows the successful development of Collins Liturgical in the UK since its inception in 1974. In terms of hardbacks about one-third of Collins's Australian sales now represents indigenous titles, including those cases, which are increasingly frequent, where Collins has purchased the Australian rights of US titles.

Another UK firm that is deeply entrenched in Australia - and, indeed, one that had, until 1980, Australian minority shareholders is <u>Associated Book Publishers</u>. As in the case of William Collins, acquisitions have played a significant part in the expansion of the group, notably the Law Book Company, control of which was obtained by Sweet & Maxwell in 1962, and on the non-legal side, the Hicks Smith Group, which had been Methuen's agents, purchased in 1964. In 1981 ABP Australia acquired from Macmillan Inc. the exclusive marketing and distribution rights in Australia for the Macmillan company (not UK Macmillan) lists (including Cassells), thereby extending ABP's interests in educational, academic and general publishing. A number of these purchases have been aimed at securing an economic scale of operations across ABP's wide range of publishing sectors, in almost all of which local publishing is an essential - and in some cases predominant - ingredient. The most recent move took place in October, 1983 and involved geographical expansion when ABP bought the well-known New Zealand firm A. H. & A. W. Reed for NZ$1.2m.

The process of achieving improved financial performance has also involved a centralization of activities to the point where the group now operates in Australia from one centre as against as many as thirteen at one stage.

In paperbacks, <u>Penguin</u> has probably succeeded best in projecting an Australian flavour to its publishing - helped by the fact that it has had a branch in Melbourne for thirty-six years. This high Australian profile is seen as furthering Penguin sales of imported books - still close to 85 per cent of the total - but also as a developing source of profit in its own right. Penguin has a total of three commissioning editors and, in contrast to some other UK-based firms, Penguin regards export prospects of Australian titles with a certain degree of optimism. This is particularly the case with children's books. It is also true that the greater emphasis on front-list publishing, which now accounts for some 30 per cent of sales against 20 per cent five years ago, while the back list sales represent 70 per cent against 80 per cent, is itself leading to increased emphasis on indigenous publishing. An interesting development announced in September 1983 was a co-publishing and agency agreement with McPhee Gribble, an enterprising small Melbourne publishing house. As a result, many of the firm's new titles are being co-published with Penguin Australia.

Routledge and Kegan Paul are one of the most recent publishers to have established a physical presence in Australia. In February 1982 a branch office was opened in Melbourne and the first Routledge title to carry the Melbourne imprint was published shortly thereafter. A UK publisher developing vigorously in Australia is Allen & Unwin, which now employs a staff of nineteen from initially one in 1976, and whose 1983 publishing programme included 60 new Australian titles, against 37 in 1982, 31 in 1981 and a mere four in 1977. In 1983 Edward Arnold (Australia) appointed a publishing manager for Australian books; the goal is to produce twelve new titles a year in the educational and technical fields. Hodder & Stoughton's excellent 1982-83 results reflected in part the good figures from their overseas companies. In fact H & S Australia and H & S New Zealand, with local publishing playing strong parts in both companies, each returned record sales. One reason given for the establishment in 1981 of Transworld Australia was that it should become the vehicle for the eventual development of indigenous publishing. The Oxford University Press, for its part, continues to pursue a vigorous local publishing programme building on its seventy-five years in Australia.

The experience of Pan Books is of a different order, however. In February 1977 Pan recruited staff and opened a publishing office in Sydney; 1980 saw the appearance of the first dozen titles in an Australian paperback list. But in mid-1983 Pan closed its local publishing department. This largely reflects the difficulties of developing from scratch a viable indigenous paperback publishing activity while at the same time limiting the financial commitment. Pan plans to continue to publish a small number of local titles each year and could at some stage revive plans to publish more extensively in Australia.

Finally, the following table brings together the statistics on a limited number of Australian subsidiaries of UK houses, differentiating between sales of Australian and imported books. There are also some developments in the way in which foreign publishers having little or no local publishing organize their sales efforts in Australia which have some interesting features.

Table 58

Estimated Sales Pattern of Selected Publishers

| | Australian titles | | Imported titles (a) | | TOTAL titles |
	($Am)	(%)	($Am)	(%)	($Am)
Penguin	2.0	17	10.0	83	12.0
Methuen (Aus)	2.3	33	4.7	67	7.0
Macmillan (Aus)	6.0	67	3.0	33	9.0
Longman Cheshire	9.0	78	2.5	22	11.5
Heinemann (Aus)	2.1	50	2.2	50	4.3

(a) Includes agencies

Faber & Faber is an example of one firm that has recently changed its Australian selling arrangements. Previously the Faber list was carried by Oxford University Press. However, as Faber's publishing programme lost some of its academic emphasis and became broader in appeal the 'fit' with OUP became less satisfactory. Consequently, in January 1982 Faber & Faber left OUP to go to Penguin Australia. On the paperback side, which is about half in value terms, Faber & Faber now have the support of the 13-strong Penguin sales force. On the hardback side the same Penguin salesmen are themselves carrying a Faber list that complements happily the Allen Lane list. More generally, Faber & Faber benefit from Penguin's proven warehousing and distribution system. The arrangement also includes a feature that represents a halfway position between a firm having its own dedicated sales force and having an impersonal agency arrangement; in the Penguin offices, Faber & Faber employ one man whose role it is to monitor Faber's business and to act as Faber's marketing man in Australia. The fact that he is an ex-Penguin employee on good terms with his erstwhile colleagues puts the seal on what would appear to be an advantageous agreement for both Faber and Penguin. In 1982, the first year of the new arrangement, sales rose 35 per cent and in 1983 the increase was of the order of 20 per cent. This performance is consistent with Penguin's reputation for sales and distribution, with one bookseller referring to Penguin Australia as 'a sort of Sebastian Coe amongst publishers'.

As noted in the following chapter on paperbacks, Pan Books have also altered their Australian selling arrangements. Since the start of 1983 they have undertaken the selling of Pan titles in some of the major centres accounting for one-third of

the market through their own sales force numbering ten.
Collins, who had previously carried the Pan list throughout
Australia, continue to sell Pan books across the other two-
thirds of the market and also remain wholly responsible for the
warehousing and distribution of all Pan titles.

Pan's move to establish its own force follows a decision
taken by Mills & Boon at the start of 1982, whereby they also
undertook the selling of their own books throughout Australia.
This was a role which Collins had previously filled; once again
Collins continue to warehouse and distribute the Mills & Boon
books.

Yet another example of a paperback publishing house choosing
to assume responsibility for the sale of its own books is
Bantam/Corgi following the establishment in March 1981 of the
subsidiary Transworld Australia. Previously Gordon & Gotch had
been the agents for both Bantam and Corgi. In late 1983, the
process was carried one step further with the establishment of
their own publishing and distribution company in New Zealand.

5.Outlook for Australian Publishing

Considerable sympathy must be felt for the frustration
experienced by Australians who found themselves enfolded in the
British Publishers' Traditional Market Agreement, the creation
of which stemmed from a visit to the USA in 1943 of three
leading UK publishers. One aspect was the financial penalty to
which a US publisher exposed himself were he to seek to break
down the volume rights sold within the traditional British
market. The UK signatories to the agreement - the great bulk of
UK publishers - agreed that unless they could acquire volume
rights covering the whole area, they would decline to publish a
book in any part of that area. In practical terms, this meant
that if an American publisher disposed of the Australian rights
of an American book to an Australian publisher, no British
publisher (who was a signatory to the agreement) would publish
that book in England or in any other part of the traditional
British market.

In 1973, the rules were relaxed to the extent that US
publishers were henceforth enabled to license Australian rights
to an Australian publisher and the rights for the rest of the
market area to a British publisher. This did not, however,
enable a US publisher to retain the Australian rights if he
wished to sell the British market rights, excluding Australia,
to a UK publisher.

It was only with the implementation of the US Federal
Anti-Trust Consent Decree in March 1976 that this obstacle to
US publishers' disposal/retention of foreign rights in the tra-
ditional British market area was removed.

Not all the frustrations of the Australian book trade have,
however, been eliminated. For example, the time-lag that often

exists between the publication of a US title and its publication in the UK, not to mention its availability in Australia, presents temptations which are not always resisted by retailers who ignore copyright and buy in copies from the USA. The situation also arises when there is a substantial gap between the US and UK prices, perhaps because the UK book is only available in hardback format at a time when the US paperback has already been published. Temptations and frustrations again flow from these circumstances, all the more so as US reviews and publicity are widely read in Australia. There is as a result a degree of pressure towards altering the copyright rules with a view to reducing these time-lags. A legal seminar is, in fact, to be convened by the Attorney-General's Department to consider copyright.

What is clear is that the whole post-war drift of regulations has been in the direction of freeing the Australian book trade of controls many have judged to be onerous. It has gone hand in hand, as has been seen, with the development of indigenous Australian publishing.

One observation that stems from the tables at the start of this chapter is not particularly comforting. The statistical evidence - and admittedly the figures can be challenged - indicates that there has been little real growth in the Australian market since the mid-1970s. What has happened, however, is that there has been a transformation of the market with the displacement of imports by local publications, particularly in the educational field. This has enabled some firms of publishers, with ambition and resources, to develop swiftly. The benefits of economies of increasing scale have furthermore enabled them to report rapid profits growth.

Looking ahead, the displacement of imports in the educational field may still have some way to go, but inevitably the task gets harder and harder, particularly if one bears in mind the fact that the import statistics include a large lump of tertiary books imported from the USA for which there is no local substitute. In addition, demographic influences only start to become a little more positive towards the end of the decade.

Nevertheless most observers anticipate a continuation of the post-war trend towards greater Australian publishing in both the educational and general fields. One likely trend is seen to be publishing which will be increasingly tailored to regional needs. Already in primary and secondary education, it is more and more the case that the particular requirements of the different states are being met. In the opinion of Angus & Robertson, the same is likely to occur to an increasing extent in general publishing, leading to the treatment of subjects in ways that suit specific geographic areas.

The extent to which the explosion in Australian-interest subjects that has occurred since the early 1970s will be prolonged is harder to determine. In the opinion of the literary agents Curtis Brown the growth of such publishing is likely to slow down, while one firm of retailers believes that the market is approaching saturation. Publishers, however, on the whole are planning for further growth and, as the Australian Book Publishers Association expressed it 'with the approach of the 1988 bicentennial celebrations there will be a heightened awareness amongst all Australians of our national culture and identity. Australian book publishers will have a significant supportive role to play in publishing titles which reflect national aspirations and contribute to the success of this important Australian occasion'.

For overseas publishers the Australian market is increasingly mature and discriminating. As a simple outlet for UK exports, Australia undoubtedly offers more limited scope than was the case some years ago thanks to changing tastes. In addition, those books for which there is a demand need to be priced and marketed in a way that takes account of a much more competitive environment. To give a specific example, one instance concerns a book priced in the UK at £6.95; this would have normally sold at a good A$20 in Australia, indicating a 65 per cent mark-up on an exchange rate at that time of A$1.75 to the £. However, the existence of a competitive US book led to a recommended Australian price of A$12.95, indicating a mark-up on the UK retail price of a mere 6 per cent. For the Australian subsidiary of the UK publisher, the delivered cost of the book in Australia worked out at A$3.61; after deducting the trade discount of 40 per cent from the recommended Australian price, they were left with a gross profit of A$4.16 per copy. This serves to highlight the wisdom of the comment that the days when two profits could be obtained on a UK book exported to Australia are well and truly passed. In the example cited above, moreover, the earnings of the Australian subsidiary from this particular title were heavily influenced by the volume of sales achieved, given the competitive pricing that was forced on it.

In the light of these observations, the examples cited earlier of UK publishers reviewing their selling arrangements – often by assuming the task themselves – and examining critically their existing systems of distribution should come as little surprise.

In the field of indigenous publishing, the further growth that is anticipated is of considerable relevance to UK publishers as they plan their development in the 1980s. Some British firms have in effect already converted themselves into Australian companies first and foremost and distributors of UK books as a secondary activity. There are others, however, whose concession to local publishing has been token or cosmetic in scale and a third category who have still to take the first steps. The indications are that an increased commitment to local publishing will prove necessary for a UK firm to protect an existing position in the Australian market – let alone benefit from the future growth of the Australian economy.

Furthermore, the importance of educational sales in the overall total and the absence of some of the sharp distinctions that exist in the UK, as between net and non-net books, suggests that a combination of educational and general strengths is a significant advantage. This is notwithstanding the earlier comments on the competitive outlook in the field of education.

The burgeoning of indigenous publishing in the non-educational area undoubtedly invites questions on profitability. Publishing for a small audience is hardly a formula for great prosperity. A key in the economics of such publishing lies, however, in obtaining the most advantageous production costs and in this respect the familiarity of Australian publishers with Hong Kong, Japanese and Singapore printers is a distinct advantage. There is also greater willingness on the part of Australian publishers to use 'packagers' as a way of avoiding the assumption of heavy fixed costs in the form of editorial wages and related overheads.

One unanswered question concerns exports where the achievements to date have been modest, with sport a possible exception. The interesting exhibition held in London in October 1983 under the title "Australian Publishing: A Decade of Achievement', to which seventy Australian publishers contributed, was the first comprehensive exhibition of Australian books to have been held abroad and may herald a more determined export effort by Australian publishers. Optimism on this score is voiced by such a person as Trevor Glover who runs Penguin's Australian operation; his views may be coloured, however, by his being part of a group with a decidedly internationalist flavour. It is also true that a continued swing to Australian-interest titles is not in itself a great spur to exports.

The crucial area must remain the domestic market, where the population trends promise significant overall growth, which should benefit, particularly, general book sales.

The Australian is, moreover, a confirmed book buyer who responds to promotion, whether it takes temporarily the form of cut-price books sold by the kilo or heavily advertised titles that carry impressive cover prices. In 1982 sales of books per head of population came to A$39, equivalent to some £24. In the United Kingdom the comparable figure was £19. Given a reasonable economic environment, the Australian market should achieve real growth, while opportunities will continue to exist for the well-managed cost-conscious firm to expand market share and increase profitability.

PAPERBACKS

1. UK Statistics

As with many other aspects of UK publishing, reliable statistics on UK paperbacks are hard to find. A fundamental problem is that of definition. The Business Monitor figures are concerned with format, so that all books not hardback, but bound in limp covers or in paper covers, are classified as paperbacks. This is the definition that governs the statistics in Table 59.

The period covered has seen a steady rise in the proportion of UK publishers' sales at current prices made up of paperbacks, from 28 per cent in 1971 to 37½ per cent in 1982. In terms of constant prices, the evidence suggests an overall reduction in book sales, reflecting a sizeable contraction in hardback sales between 1976 and 1982, the fall being particularly marked in 1981. At the same time, sales of paperbacks adjusted for inflation have shown some growth over the full 1972-82 period and in particular advanced briskly in 1980 and further in 1981. This would suggest trading down from hardbacks to paperbacks, in the context of a difficult economic situation.

The point needs to be made, however, that use in the table of the Book Price Index leads to more depressed figures of real sales than would have been the case had the Retail Price Index or The Booksellers' Index been used (see Table 23). One serious blemish of the Book Price Index is that it does not cover academic and institutional sales.

In the face of this baffling mass of often contradictory evidence, the fact that is not in dispute is that paperbacks have had an above-average performance.

In contrast to the Business Monitor statistics, those collected by the Publishers Association are restricted to 'mass-market' paperbacks, currently published by fourteen paperback houses. This focuses primarily on paperbacks that are produced in above-average runs and sold in non-conventional, as well as traditional, retail book outlets. Publication of a new series provides a welcome improvement in the statistics, but they only cover the period starting in 1981. For earlier years the decision was taken to rely on the statistics assembled by the Book Marketing Council and periodically published in The Bookseller. While these certainly fall short of perfection, it is to be hoped that there is a degree of consistency to them, which makes them useful in the indication they give of shifts in direction and rates of change even if the absolute figures may be somewhat suspect. Table 60 is restricted to publishers' home sales.

Table 59

UK Publishers' Hardback & Paperback Sales - Current & 1972 Prices

| (£million) | Current Prices | | | | Paperbacks as % of total |
	Hardback	Paperback	Royalties	TOTAL	
1982*	474.1	303.2	29.0	806.4	37.6
1981	460.2	303.9	25.5	789.6	38.5
1980	437.5	255.4	22.3	715.2	35.7
1979	387.1	210.7	19.5	617.4	34.1
1978	345.6	189.8	17.3	552.7	34.3
1977	287.2	165.0	14.8	467.0	35.3
1976	254.6	138.6	15.1	408.3	33.9
1975	221.7	110.5	10.2	342.4	32.3
1974	186.2	85.7	9.7	281.5	30.4
1973	152.8	68.7	8.5	230.1	29.9
1972	141.8	63.5	6.3	211.5	30.0
1971	127.9	52.7	6.0	186.6	28.2

Constant Prices 1972=100

	Hardback	Paperback	TOTAL+
1982*	78.1	111.6	88.5
1981	84.9	125.3	97.4
1980	95.1	124.1	104.1
1979	97.9	119.0	104.4
1978	96.6	118.5	103.3
1977	93.2	119.6	101.3
1976	100.5	122.3	107.3
1975	101.6	113.1	105.2
1974	107.7	110.7	108.6
1973	103.5	104.0	103.6
1972	100.0	100.0	100.0
1971	NA	NA	NA

* Provisional   + Excluding royalties
Note: These figures have not been grossed up for incomplete coverage. The deflator used to arrive at constant prices has been the Book Price Index.
Sources: Business Monitor; Publishers Association Quarterly Statistical Bulletin, September 1983

Table 60

Publishers' Net Mass-Market Paperback Sales in the UK

| | Value (£thousands) | | | Units (thousands) | | |
	Adult	Children's	TOTAL	Adult	Children's	TOTAL
New Series						
1982	63,285	9,207	72,492	88,763	16,889	105,652
1981	59,636	9,589	69,225	88,402	18,524	106,926
Old Series						
1981	64,863	9,265	74,128	90,943	21,038	111,981
1980	57,539	8,350	65,889	94,004	22,665	116,669
1979	51,410	7,913	59,323	98,923	24,324	123,247
1978	45,578	6,402	51,980	98,693	21,111	119,804
1977	35,086	5,512	40,598	88,279	20,547	108,826
1976	30,654	5,783	36,437	87,978	22,650	110,628
1975	22,740	4,351	27,091	83,789	22,287	106,076

Sources: New Series - Quarterly Statistical Bulletin, The Publishers Association, June, 1983; Old Series - Book Marketing Council of The Publishers Association

The table indicates that mass-market paperback sales in the UK by value increased two and three-quarter times between 1975 and 1981, with adult titles almost trebling and children's titles more than doubling. In unit terms a peak was reached in 1979, while over the two subsequent years there was an 8 per cent reduction in sales of adult paperbacks, and one of 14 per cent in sales of children's paperbacks. The 1982 figures show a 4½ per cent increase in value and a 1 per cent drop in volume; once again children's books underperformed.

Within the limitations of the table - it is confined to home sales and covers a period of seven years - a clear conclusion to be drawn is that mass-market paperbacks have not been a growth sector in recent experience, especially since 1979. If this is related to Table 59, which covers total paperbacks, the evidence points on the other hand to gains in non-mass-market paperbacks, notably educational and trade; included within the latter are the large format imprints, variously called B format and trade paperbacks which have proliferated in the last two to three years. This is discussed later in the present chapter.

Educational and Public Library Demand for Paperbacks

Direct statistical evidence of the growth of educational and public library demand for paperbacks is not available. However, a report published in 1983 by the Centre for Library and Information Management (CLAIM) on the Use of Paperbacks in Public Libraries in the United Kingdom confirmed the coming of age of paperbacks. Considerations that have led to a marked shift towards them in the UK public library system include:

(a) The need to get maximum mileage out of book funds which in recent experience have typically been cut in real terms and often also in nominal terms.

(b) The concurrent improvement in the physical characteristics of many paperbacks whose durability can moreover be enhanced in a variety of ways. One study suggested that the average life of paperbacks without reinforcement might amount to 20 issues, while reinforcement could extend this to a range of 30-60 issues. Measured in terms of cost per issue, most forms of reinforcement can be justified against the costs per issue of an untreated paperback.

(c) The increasing number of books that now only appear in paperback format, which has the effect of leaving the library purchaser who wants such a title with no option but to accept it in paperback; on one estimate close to 40 per cent of new paperback publications are not available in hardback.

(d) Simultaneously, reviewers are becoming much less dismissive of books in paperback format than they were.

(e) Recognition on the part of many librarians that paperbacks appeal very much more to the younger reader than do hardbacks;

(f) they are also often easier to handle by the elderly.

The CLAIM study suggests that this breakthrough for paperbacks is of relatively recent date. It is also uneven, with some libraries reporting as little as 3 per cent of volumes acquired have been paperbacks and others as much as 45 per cent. Alan Longworth, President of the Library Association in 1981, is quoted as saying 'we in libraries have scarcely begun to come to terms with the paperback revolution but the diminishing purchasing power of all our book funds is inevitably forcing us to buy fewer hardbacks, and publishers will not be slow to react to this situation'.

Another way of approaching the subject is through the library suppliers themselves dealing in paperbacks. The largest of these is Books for Students which forms part of the Websters Group. It was set up in 1966 for the purpose of supplying paperbacks to schools and public libraries; by 1982, its turnover amounted to some £4½m, with public libraries accounting for 55 per cent, and schools 45 per cent. The current annual rate of sales is closer to £6m. Management finds clear evidence that substantial further growth will be achieved in both markets.

2. US Statistics

Turning to the United States, rather more extensive statistical information is available to give flesh to the term 'paperback revolution', though there are some difficulties of classification as exemplified in the disparities between the old series and new series in Table 61.

Table 61

Selected US Paperback Statistics - Publishers' Sales

	Old Series		
($million)	1963	1967	1972
Adult Trade	126	188	353
of which,			
Hardback	109	156	273
Paperback	17	32	80
Paperback as %	13	17	23
Juvenile Trade	NA	NA	NA
Mass-market paperbacks**	87	130	253

	New Series							
($million)	1972	1977	1978	1979	1980	1981	1982	1987+
Adult Trade	332	670	799	854	1,044	1,180	1,177	2,179
of which,								
Hardback	252	501	594	627	750	858	797	1,250
Paperback	80	169	205	227	294	322	380	929
Paperback as %	24	25	26	27	28	27	32	43
Juvenile Trade	111	162	185	191	229	248	258	486
of which,								
Hardback	107	136	147	157	177	194	199	397
Paperback	4	26	38	34	52	54	59	89
Paperback as %	4	16	21	18	23	22	23	18
Mass-market paperbacks**	253	543	609	676	761	882	998	2,170

Note: Including Exports. + Forecast. ** Includes non-rack-sized
Sources: Association of American Publishers Book Industry
Trends, 1983, Book Industry Study Group Inc; Publishers Weekly

One of the most impressive statistics serving to illustrate the development of the paperback is the virtually uninterrupted rise in the percentage of adult trade books in paperback format from a mere 13 per cent in 1963 to 32 per cent in 1982. The juvenile trade figures show an even more rapid rate of growth, but from extremely low levels. Turning to mass-market paperbacks, sales have risen elevenfold between 1963 and 1982, which is more than twice the near fivefold sales increase achieved by the US book publishing trade as a whole (see Table 42).

Looking five years ahead, the latest Book Industry Study Group forecasts indicate a continued strong swing to paperbacks in adult trade books. In juveniles, while the absolute numbers are expected to continue to rise, the paperback proportion is set to slip back. This has been a volatile series in the past and the quantities are not vast, so that this suggested reversal may well not have great statistical significance.

3. Trade Paperbacks

Rising institutional demand for paperbacks was cited earlier as a growth point in paperbacks. The other - of totally different character - was the so-called 'trade paperback' or B format paperback. This is a phenomenon that has been particularly marked in the United States, some aspects of which are discussed below.

Trade Paperbacks - USA

The special report entitled The Burgeoning of Trade Paperbacks issued in August 1982 by the US trade journal Publishers Weekly, declared that 'there is no doubt that it's the fastest-growing and therefore the most exciting area of publishing at the moment'. It was also said to be the source simultaneously of the principal complaint about 'non-books' - and of the best hope for the future of literacy. Finally, quoting a publisher, the mass-market trade paperback was described as 'a precarious goldmine'.

In the opinion of Roger Straus of Farrar Straus Giroux, a genuine trade paperback has the following characteristics. It follows a clothbound edition priced at, say, $12.95-25.00 and is itself priced at perhaps $6.95-8.95. The initial print run typically falls between 7,500 and 15,000, and the book is sold on full sale or return through traditional book outlets and is carried by the traditional hardback sales force. The discount to the trade ranges from 40 per cent to 49 per cent and returns require the physical shipment of the book rather than the stripping of covers as in mass-market paperbacks. The proportions returned are closer to the experience of trade hardbacks than of mass-market paperbacks.

Where the trade paperback is a reprint of a hardback, the latter will have borne the promotion costs (and will have attracted the reviews), thereby helping towards a low trade paperback cover price. Authors' royalties are in the 6 per cent, 7½ per cent, 10 per cent range, rather than the 10 per cent, 12½ per cent, 15 per cent range for hardbacks. Where the trade paperback rights are sold, royalties are divided evenly between the original publisher and the author. Where the original publisher 'trade paperbacks' one of his own authors, the author does not receive an advance, but earns his royalties as the sales are achieved.

A trade paperback that satisfies these criteria fulfils the trade paperback publisher's goal of meeting the needs of a public that is neither in the market for the hardback nor in that for the mass-market paperback. A case in point is Richard Nixon's autobiography, which was published seriatim in hardback, trade paperback and mass-market paperback.

But, increasingly, these criteria are not being satisfied. The most frequent qualification to the Straus blueprint is that the trade paperback is an original which, if successful, will subsequently be published for the mass market. In such cases, it takes the place of the hardback, but the chances of success on original publication are believed to be enhanced through a relatively low cover price and by a quality image that makes the title an acceptable alternative to a hardback in the eyes of the book-buying public and the library market. But what will often distinguish a trade paperback of this kind from a comparable hardback is that it frequently forms part of a separate list or imprint. This in turn opens up the possibility of paperback-style marketing and publishing with lead titles being chosen and then promoted together with the establishment of a steady flow of new titles at a rate of x per month. In this example, we have moved a long way from the concept of a paperback reprint of a hardback of the kind envisaged by Roger Straus. The numbers are different, but the target audience continues unchanged - the patrons of traditional book outlets - and it is the sales force that deals with such accounts that remains responsible for the sales effort.

A third aspect of trade paperback publishing in the United States is somewhat confusingly described as mass-market trade paperback publishing. This is undertaken by the mass-market houses, is based on a high proportion of originals (75 per cent in the case of Ballantine, between 60 per cent and 70 per cent for Warner Books and currently over 50 per cent for Bantam), involves print runs that start in the 100,000s and is based on sales through such mass-market outlets as discount stores, supermarkets, drug stores, airports etc. using the mass-market independent distributors and the publishing house's mass-market sales force. Coverage is selective, however, the retail prices are well above those of conventional mass-market paperbacks, while the display in the retail outlets often involves special racking to accommodate non-standard formats. Subsequent to publication as a mass-market trade paperback, a successful title will quite often be issued as a mass-market paperback in a standard rack size.

As is frequently the case in publishing, whether in the USA or the UK, it is difficult to supply statistical evidence of developments in the industry. At the retail end, the US chain Waldenbooks found that, in 1982, trade paperback sales exceeded mass-market paperback sales and also hardcover sales. The B. Dalton Bookseller chain, for its part, also saw trade paperback sales in 1982 exceed hardback sales for the first time. In 1975 they were less than 10 per cent of total sales, in 1982 they were 28 per cent; John Schulz, Vice-President, has predicted that they would stay the largest element, partly because most computer books are in that format. And within the institutional market, Publishers Weekly reports estimates by several librarians that 15-25 per cent of their book funds are currently being spent on trade paperbacks, strong evidence that the paperback format has received institutional acceptance.

Trade Paperbacks - UK

UK trade paperbacks have a long history if they are defined as quality paperbacks. A more restrictive definition that emphasizes their format takes one back to some large format Penguins in the post-war years, Granada's Paladins dating from 1970, Pan's Picadors from 1972 and King Penguins which are now four years old. Since 1982 numerous trade paperback or B format imprints have been launched or their imminent launch has been announced. These include Sphere's Abacus, which is over two years old, Hutchinson's Vermilion, started in October 1982, Hutchinson's Arena launched in April 1983, Hamlyn's Zenith in March 1983, Unwin's Counterpoint in April 1983, Corgi's Black Swan in the autumn of 1983, Chatto's The Hogarth Press in February 1984 and Hamish Hamilton Paperbacks in the spring of 1984.

A characteristic of the development of trade paperbacks in the UK has been that it has typically involved the creation of specific imprints, leading to a regular pattern of publication. Hamlyn's Zenith, for instance, started with the simultaneous launch of five titles, followed by two new titles a month. Corgi also aims at two new titles a month, normally one fiction and one reprint. By their being enshrined in an imprint, a common identity is given to the individual titles and the expectation is that the list as it is gradually built up acts in its own right as a stimulus to sales. Typically, initial print runs are in the region of 7,000-15,000.

In trade paperbacks, an intriguing innovation has been the January 1984 launch by Picador of its own hardback list under the Picador Hardback imprint. Initially at least hardback and paperback titles are being published simultaneously, while the character of the books reflects the 'determined eclecticism' of the paperback list. This move into hardbacks is a further example of the hardback/paperback divide being broken down. It also illustrates the need that some publishers increasingly feel to be able to offer an author a complete package, and, more generally, is a recognition that the special standing of the hardback format retains commercial significance.

In terms of subject, trade paperbacks were first seen as particularly suitable vehicles for non-fiction. In the case of Paladin, the aim was to create 'a non-fiction imprint for the intelligent reader that was comprehensive in its range, popular in its appeal, alert to the interests and ideas currently in vogue, produced in larger format with good clean typography and interesting, arresting covers'. At its launch, Picador promised the public 'readable, revealing and highly stimulating titles written by the world's top writers exploring essentially contemporary themes'. More than ten years later these prospectuses still carry weight, except that up-market non-fiction is of increasing importance. Looking further ahead, mass-market trade paperback fiction may have a future if American experience proves relevant to the UK.

A glance at the existing trade paperback lists reveals a mixture of originals and reprints, the latter coming from both the hardback list of the originating publishing house and the lists of other firms. In fact, one of the main roles that trade paperbacks are beginning to play is that of stimulating backlist publishing through the combined impact of attractive retail prices and effective promotion.

At this stage, the future of trade paperbacks in the United Kingdom must remain an open question. One difficulty lies in attempting, through a trade name, to further sales to a consuming public that has in the past shown itself to be remarkably imprint-unconscious - barring such well-known exceptions as Penguin and Mills & Boon. An influence, however, working powerfully in their favour is that their development remains grounded on the swing of book buyers to paperbacks. Also on commercial grounds, publication through imprints or series increases the chances of review and helps with the marketing. On balance a minimum expectation may be that sales growth of trade paperbacks may compensate for any contraction of comparable hardback sales. The UK publisher of trade hardbacks who chooses to ignore the trade paperback phenomenon could therefore be running considerable risks.

4. Mass Market Paperbacks

UK Mass-Market Paperback Publishers

The discussion has illustrated a number of different trends affecting paperbacks. The statistics highlight the depression in sales in real terms. Industry figures are necessarily weighted towards the mass-market section of paperback publishing where demand has been particularly weak. At the same time, there is clear evidence of rising institutional acceptance of the paperback format and there is a great blossoming of activity centred on trade paperbacks.

If one moves from the industry level to the company level, it is interesting to note differences in the experience of individual publishers and also how managements have responded to industry trends. The following comments relate primarily to mass-market publishers, starting with Penguin - which, it must be admitted, is a special case given its unique characteristics.

Table 62

Recent Profits Record of Penguin Publishing Group

Year to 31 December (£thousands)	1975	1976	1977	1978
Turnover	17,248	18,698	18,935	22,673
Pre-tax profits	1,823	2,776	1,409	1,525
As % of turnover	10.6	14.8	7.4	6.7

Year to 31 December (£thousands)	1979	1980	1981	1982
Turnover	27,725	36,127	47,254	56,214
Pre-tax profits	(381)	242	3,966	5,636
As % of turnover	-	0.7	8.4	10.0

Note: In September 1979, Viking Penguin Inc. ceased being an associate and became a subsidiary.

In 1979, the then recently appointed Chief Executive Peter Mayer saw one of the problems as lying in a decline in front-list publishing in general, especially in fiction, leading to excessive dependence on the back list which itself was suffering a natural ageing process and was not being rejuvenated through the addition of new titles. At the same time, editors had come to think of themselves as independent publishers, making editorial decisions that only made economic sense when generous assumptions were made of: (a) initial subscriptions; (b) group sales; and (c) continuing back list sales. Too many books were appearing, therefore, for which the domestic market on its own provided inadequate support. In addition, as Peter Mayer expresses it, false notions of what constituted mass-market sales were made, based on facile notions of format and price. And, lastly, specious democratic principles prevailed when it came to spending on promotion with the result that the available funds were thinly distributed.

The marketing department was divided into two parts, leading to a high degree of specialization, the promotion and advertising side on the one hand, the press and author/tour side on the other. What was judged most damaging was the disassociation of the editorial and cover art element (the so-called creative side) from marketing and sales (the so-called business side). This was at the heart of the decision to move to new offices, where the staff were intermingled.

In the subsequent four years, front list mass market fiction publishing has come to enjoy considerable support. This is furthermore helped by a selective pattern of expenditure on promotion, with the result that lead titles receive a far larger share of the budget. The numbers of new titles were initially reduced so as to eliminate the more extreme examples of minority publishing.

Penguin's backlist which Mayer originally cut back from 5,000 to 4,200 titles is now again over 5,000, but the editorial mix is slightly different, as to format, packaging and pricing. Many titles have had their cover prices raised by factors of two to three, usually in relationship to format changes; these higher cover prices have made retention of backlist a more economic proposition. This applies particularly to the Pelican-type book, and literary fiction, where the reader's specific need makes his demand comparatively price inelastic. The back list now accounts for 75 per cent of sales against 80 per cent previously, still a level that sets Penguin apart from others in the industry.

As the table indicates, the nadir of Penguin's fortunes came in 1979 and 1980. In 1981, Penguin sold 10 per cent fewer volumes than three years previously, in line with industry trends, but made a healthy profit against a significant loss. Results in 1982 confirmed this improvement with profits up 42 per cent on a sales increase of 19 per cent. For the first half of 1983, Group profits amounted to £1.47m against a mere £21,000 the previous year, ensuring a further profits rise for the year as a whole.

As indicated in the note to Table 62, Viking Penguin's results have been fully consolidated since the end of 1979. If these are taken out of the 1981 and 1982 figures, Penguin's success in restoring margins is revealed more clearly - with the return on sales in 1981, 10.9 per cent and in 1982, 11.8 per cent.

Pan Books, second in size to Penguin among UK paperback publishers, presents the picture of a group whose profits were better sustained than were those at Penguin. However, by 1980 profits were standing at one-third of the levels achieved in the period 1976-78. It is true, however, that some exceptional items have weighed on results, notably the costs associated with the proposed distribution centre at Basingstoke. This was announced in 1979 and the decision was reversed in 1980 leading to exceptional pre-tax charges of some £150,000 in that year. The intention was then to move distribution from Macmillans at Basingstoke to Collins at Bishopbriggs. This decision was in turn reversed, following a new agreement with Macmillans; such changes of direction naturally had an adverse impact on trading results for 1981. The first half of 1982 witnessed, however, a sharp improvement with pre-tax profits rising to £717,000 from the depressed level of £288,000 in the first half of 1981, while the full-year figure was double the total for 1981. The improvement persisted in 1983, with first half pre-tax profits amounting to £984,000.

Table 63

Pre-Tax Profits of Pan

(£thousands)	1975	1976	1977	1978
Turnover	7,953	9,908	10,663	12,543
Pre-tax profits	1,077	1,266	1,188	1,203
Margins (%)	13.5	12.8	11.1	9.6

(£thousands)	1979	1980	1981	1982
Turnover	13,922	15,986	17,232	15,787*
Pre-tax profits	717	420	510	1,054
Margins (%)	5.2	2.6	3.0	+

* Excluding six months of Australian sales. + Not comparable
Source: Derived from William Collins & Sons annual accounts

In the light of the dull sales figures for the industry as a whole, this is an impressive turnaround. If reflects margin improvement stemming from the decline of sterling, a rise in paperback prices that outstripped the inflation in manufacturing costs, and the persistent application of better 'housekeeping' practices, one aspect of which has been lower stocks and hence lower interest charges.

For the longer term, the decision over distribution arrangements is important. The original intention had been to invest some £4m in a new centre at Basingstoke comprising a warehouse, offices and an electronic data-processing department, due for completion towards the end of 1981. This was to coincide with the end of the existing arrangements for Pan's distribution from part of Macmillan's Basingstoke centre. The view taken by Simon Master, the new managing director, was that if money in those amounts was to be spent, it would be better that it should be spent on the publishing side and that a policy of sub-contracting 'mechanical' tasks such as warehousing and distribution - in addition to printing and binding - was essential if resources were to be allocated efficiently. The situation at Pan undoubtedly has some special features, notably the limited amount of internal financial resources due to a policy of high dividend distributions to its three shareholders, Collins, Heinemann and Macmillan: finance would therefore have had to have come through outside borrowings (possibly in part from its three shareholders). Nonetheless, the decision of a major publisher to renounce plans to undertake its own distribution could point the way to other publishers. While it may increase the operating gearing of a company, it encourages a dedication to the main activity of publishing. It is also consistent with a trend apparent in many industries where the computer has taken the 'magic' out of many processes that previously required individual attention. Once efficiently programmed, it is a great leveller.

A feature in the development of Pan over the past ten years or so, which is of major significance, is the steady increase in the number of Pan originals (ie titles not previously published in hardback or paperback) and decline in its dependence on the paperback rights of other publishers' hardback titles. This has meant a substantial investment on the editorial side which now numbers eleven, including two editorial directors, five commissioning editors and four desk editors. In 1982 Pan published a total of 288 titles (157 new books, 131 new editions), of which about half represented Pan originals. In the early 1970s the proportion would have been little more than 10 per cent.

More recently, an important ingredient in Pan's programme for profits recovery has been a shift in sales policy through the withdrawal of overseas agency agreements with other firms. The aim, wherever possible, is for Pan to be directly responsible for its sales performance, ie the reverse of the sub-contracting goal that applies to the mechanical tasks mentioned above. In Australia, Pan has established a sales force of ten who, from the start of 1983, have been carrying its books to all but the geographically remote areas and those outlets that are typically serviced by wholesalers. Collins, which previously had the entire Pan agency, continues to serve these areas. The ware-

111

housing remains with Collins. In 1983, the first year of operation of the new arrangements, unit sales increased by about 10 per cent above 1982. This compares with a generally static performance in mass-market paperbacks in Australia. It is attributed to the benefits to Pan of having control of its own promotional efforts, as well as to having its own sales force.

In an earlier move, Pan had undertaken its own selling on the Continent from the start of 1982. This involves a dedicated sales team of two and replaces the previous arrangements whereby the Collins paperback sales force on the Continent carried both Pan and Fontana. One reason given for the new arrangements was that the editorial character of the two firms was changing, leading to their lists becoming increasingly competitive and less complementary. This reinforced the fundamental aim that Pan should seek to control its own destiny in respect of sales. In 1982 cash sales in Europe increased by 35 per cent and in 1983 by about 10 per cent.

Turning to other UK mass-market paperback houses, the available information is more limited, but the struggle in the short term has been to keep costs aligned to weak sales, hence a succession of retrenchments and rationalizations. On a longer time horizon, the aim of most of the medium-sized imprints remains to achieve an economic scale of operations. The level of sales that is judged to be required has been estimated by various paperback publishers as falling between £4m and £8m. In this connection, the purchase by Hodder & Stoughton in 1981 of New English Library from the Times Mirror Group linked NEL and Coronet, thereby making them a sizeable force in the industry. At Hutchinson the unification in 1980 of the Arrow paperback and the Geographia/Nicholson map and guide sales force went some way towards establishing a viable unit. In mid-1983 Hutchinson took the process one stage further by buying, for an undisclosed sum, the loss-making Hamlyn Paperbacks, thereby raising total paperback turnover from £5½m to a figure approaching £8m. A very much larger merger took place earlier in the year, when Collins bought Granada Publishing which added £11½m of turnover (about 60 per cent from paperbacks) to Collins's Group total of £80m. In both instances one of the extra attractions was the prospect of increased throughput for their own manufacturing and distribution operations.

Of the other mass-market paperback imprints, Thomson's Sphere, started in 1967, and BPCC's Futura, launched in 1973, have been a frequent cause for concern to their owners. The difficulties experienced by these and other mass-market paperback publishers have not prevented new entrants into the field, however. The American Avon Books is a case in point. Having previously sold to British paperback publishers UK and Commonwealth rights on its titles, Avon announced in mid-1982 that henceforth it would retain volume rights and distribute direct into the UK, using for that purpose LSP Books, a distributor based in Goldalming, Surrey. At the time Avon was reported as seeing real growth in such markets as South Africa, Australia, New Zealand and the UK. In May 1983, Avon announced a further, and more ambitious, step in its penetration of the UK market, following an agreement with Bantam's UK subsidiary, Corgi Books, which replaced that with LSP Books. Under the new arrangement Corgi and Avon co-publish 'important' Avon titles, chiefly in the romance field, under the joint Corgi/Avon imprint. In addition, Corgi has the right to select other Avon titles either for co-publication or for import and distribution. The link with Avon followed an agreement in Australia, under which Transworld Australia (a subsidiary of Corgi Books) distributed Avon titles in that country.

Another new entrant had been Associated Book Publishers. By 1976, ABP had seen its investment in paperbacks for the mass-market increase significantly, with titles being drawn from ABP's own back list and from other hardcover houses, all published under the Methuen Paperbacks imprint. At the end of the year it was decided to establish a specialist unit for mass-market paperbacks with the launch of Magnum a mass-market adult paperback imprint (followed in 1979 by the launch of Magnet, a mass-market children's paperback imprint). This eventually involved the appointment of three acquiring editors and the creation of a specialist paperback sales force of about ten. Previously editorial decisions on paperbacks had been taken by editors whose main function was in respect of hardbacks, while paperbacks had been sold by the Group's hardcover trade book sales force. A rate of publication of up to 10 titles a month was set and a separate mass-market paperback promotion budget was established. Funds were made available for advances to authors.

By 1979, management reported that Magnum had grown steadily to establish a list of middlebrow, commercial authors in fiction and non-fiction, including practical books, historical romance, crime, science fiction, fantasy and war. Magnet Books' main source of titles was Methuen's Children's Books. In the ensuing years, the Group's annual reviews of its activities emphasized the competitive character of mass-market paperbacks and, starting in 1980, the seriously adverse effects of the recession. In 1981 Magnum's publishing programme was curtailed, and in 1982 the decision was taken once again to amalgamate all adult paperback publishing under the Methuen imprint, while continuing to preserve the separate identity of the children's imprint, Magnet. The mass-market paperback sales force was disbanded and the paperback commissioning editors absorbed into Methuen's own editorial department. The total investment that had been made in Magnum amounted to £1.7m.

This brings one to a consideration of the implications for the relationship between paperback and hardback publishing of some of the general trends that are increasingly apparent in the industry.

5. The Changing Relationships of Hardbacks to Paperbacks

The statistics at the start of this chapter that demonstrate the rising proportion of books sold - whether in the UK or in the USA - in a paperback format mean in fact that most publishers are now publishers of paperbound books.

At one level such paperback 'publishing' might more properly be regarded as the result of a manufacturing decision: it involves the simultaneous production of so many copies of a specific title in hardback (to satisfy the needs of a residual core of buyers who still insist on that format as well as to maximize the chances of serious reviews) and a much larger number of copies in paperback priced at perhaps 60 per cent to 75 per cent of the hardback edition. The audience aimed at is, in this instance, very largely the same as when only a hardback edition might have been contemplated, and the overall numbers published do not differ substantially from what might have been the figure previously. The methods by which the title is sold remain unchanged.

Decisions of a 'publishing' rather than a 'manufacturing' character start to be made when overall numbers are raised and the paperback list price relative to that of the hardback is lowered. While this still involves sales through the same outlets, the economics become substantially different with the broadening of the target. A further step in this same direction might come when publication only takes place in a paperback format - a trade paperback original is an obvious example. The same is true of a reprint which is decided on in paperback rather than hardback form.

A further accentuation of the paperback 'publishing' decision comes with the broadening of the audience aimed at to include some of those serviced through the non-traditional outlets. One instance of this arises with the increased use of book wholesalers who provide publishers with access to retail outlets that fall outside their normal distribution pattern. And finally, there is the full-blown mass-marketing of a title, normally previously published in hardback - or conceivably in trade paperback.

Enumerating different aspects of paperback publishing in this fashion helps to illustrate the point made earlier, namely the virtual impossibility of any publishing house of any size not to be engaged these days in some aspects at least of paperbacks as well as hardbacks. The old sharp distinction has gone in the commercial world. It may still persist in the minds of some of the more conservative authors for whom there is a world of difference still between being 'paperbacked' (a humdrum event) and 'hardbacked' (an elevating experience). It certainly remains in the attitudes of many newspaper and periodical reviewers who still fail to notice paperback editions.

It is true that a UK hardback publisher may chose to minimize his direct exposure to paperbacks by selling wherever possible the paperback reprint rights, whether for publication as trade paperbacks, as 'conventional' paperbacks sold through traditional book outlets, but lacking the imprint approach of trade paperbacks, or as mass-market paperbacks. The dangers in such a policy are that the publisher may find himself increasingly trying to sell a product for which demand is falling (the hardback) or where he is at a competitive disadvantage (offering paperback reprint rights on titles where competition is coming from other houses' paperback originals). It is in the mass-market area, which continues to require exceptional promotional and selling skills, that the distinctions between hardback and paperback remain sharp.

This blurring of distinctions is having a number of consequences at various levels. In paperback wholesaling, a company such as Bookwise is making a considerable effort at developing its business with the public library market, where it has links with virtually all local authorities, with schools throughout the country where it has helped set up and now services over 6,000 paperback shops in schools, and with the traditional bokselling outlets. This reflects a belief that its skills are not simply relevant to CTN chains (confectionery, tobacco and news chains). Also, the disappointing performance of UK mass-market paperbacks in recent years, which emerges from the statistics already given, is pushing Bookwise towards emphasizing new markets.

Within UK mass-market publishing houses, the distinction has so far been preserved between the mass-market sales force (in those instances where a firm has an in-house mass-market imprint) and the sales force selling to conventional book outlets; this also entails separate promotion budgets.

At the editorial level, however, there have been a number of changes in several publishing houses. At Penguin, the earlier pattern of having separate editors in charge of imprints was abandoned with the appointment of Peter Carson as the person in overall charge of UK editorial, while beneath him are the various editors. The recent reorganization at Viking Penguin has also led to the adult hardcover and paperback divisions being joined together under the same management team. In Peter Mayer's words 'it anticipates a further diminution of the importance traditionally attached to physical format per se in general book publishing'.

At Associated Book Publishers, the company has reverted to its earlier practice of having the same editors publish in hardback and paperback; one result has been that the amount of buying-in of adult paperback rights is now more selective and, in particular, there is less emphasis on purely category fiction. On the selling side, the same travellers carry both formats, while penetration of the mass market is achieved through the wholesalers. Promotion of adult paperbacks is no longer undertaken at the level of the imprint but on a book by book basis, though paperback lists are still prepared.

115

ABP's present approach to paperbacks does not merely reflect their earlier failure to establish a mass-market imprint. As Michael Turner, the Group's chief executive, argues, the market is by no means as polarized as it was previously. While in their experience it has long been possible in the case of exceptional titles for mass-market sales figures to be achieved without going through a specialist mass-market house (the Winnie the Pooh books in the 1970s for instance), such opportunities are becoming much more widely spread. ABP's range of recent paperback bestsellers covers conventional 'pocket book' titles (Eye-Witness Falklands), 'trade paperbacks' (Chocolate) and the Dead Cat series which has sold over three-quarters of a million copies. This attitude of self-sufficiency in paperback publishing across the whole gamut of sales possibilities is again illustrated by the 1983 publication in paperback by Methuen Paperbacks of The Secret Diary of Adrian Mole, aged 13¾, rather than by an acknowledged, outside, mass-market paperback house.

Perhaps, however, the most interesting development relates to a decision taken by Faber & Faber, a publishing house whose initiatives in a number of areas are commented on in this report. In analysing its business, management found, somewhat to its surprise, that Faber Paperbacks, which stem from the pre-war Faber Library cheap reprints, had developed to the point where some 45 per cent of titles in print were in paperback and 55 per cent in hardback (with, moreover, the swing towards paperbacks gathering pace). The more rapid growth of paperbacks to date is shown in their rise as a percentage of total sales by value over a three-year period from 41 per cent to 58 per cent (and in units from 68 per cent to 77 per cent), matched by a fall in the proportion accounted for by hardbacks from 56 per cent to 40 per cent. Finally, at last year-end, stocks of paperbacks exceeded in value stocks of hardbacks. The inescapable conclusion was that Faber & Faber had ceased to be a hardback house with a paperback arm and had become primarily a paperback publisher with a hardback list.

An intriguing feature of this development - and one that speaks loudly for the strength of the forces in the market place supporting paperbacks - is that this shift should have occurred within a firm that had previously had no formal paperback policy.

There are, naturally enough, some special features to the situation at Fabers, which will serve to limit analogies with other firms. As publishers of poetry, they have a long tradition of paperback originals, which has undoubtedly helped to encourage paperback publication within other areas of the list. The absence of a formal paperback policy has meant that the great bulk of their paperback publishing activity has involved simultaneous hardback/paperback publication of their own titles or reprints from the Faber & Faber back list, rather than the purchase from outside publishers of paperback reprint rights.

Finally, the nature of the Faber list is such that its paperbacks include not only 'egghead' and special-interest titles but also books that sell in mass-market quantities (Lawrence Durrell and William Golding) without having to be marketed as mass-market titles.

Management's readiness to accept the changes of structure and practice that flow from a recognition of the new character of the firm reflects a number of judgements. Firstly that each new generation of readers will be paperback rather than hardback oriented, thereby reinforcing the existing swing. Secondly, were the present pattern of a rising proportion of paperback royalties that goes to the author rather than the publisher to persist, subsidiary rights income could be an uncertain source of profit growth for hardback publishers. Thirdly, it can be demonstrated on a number of reasonable assumptions that in-house paperbacking – or, more properly, exploiting volume rights under one roof – is more profitable both to the author and to the publisher than would be the case where paperback royalties are earned and divided between the hardback publisher and the author. This is not to deny, however, the problems of adjustment that are called for. This is particularly true of the sales side, where logic would seem to call for the establishment of a specific mass-market sales capability so that titles with a broad appeal can be exploited to the full. Also, for a hardback house, the cash flow advantages of known paperback advances now rather than uncertain profits tomorrow can prove a compelling argument.

The point that only experience will resolve is whether a move of this kind needs to be regarded as financially defensive or aggressive. The more pessimistic view is that increased paperback sales will mean lower margins (higher returns, bigger discounts, lower list prices more than offsetting increased turnover) and perhaps little change in profits. The more optimistic view is that this will only prove true of a hardback house that is an unwilling convert to present-day realities. If, on the other hand, these are embraced, and the conversion is profound, this becomes an aggressive move that promises profits growth.

Finally, a discussion along these lines cannot conclude on a note that suggests that paperbacks have already won the day and that hardbacks are in headlong retreat. Some hardback publishers are counter-attacking vigorously and challenging one of paperbacks' main claims to attention, namely price. In the UK, Paul Hamlyn is most closely identified with this battle. While Octopus publishes a considerable number of paperbacks, the bulk of its output is made up of hardbacks. These are characterized by their high standards of production, a strong emphasis on colour and excellent value for money. Low unit costs are achieved by large volume sales, furthered by an international marketing effort with some 40 per cent of sales going to overseas customers. These big volumes reflect Paul

117

Hamlyn's repeated strokes of genius in linking Octopus to retail chains across the world which themselves are growing rapidly and within whose business books are an expanding force.

The virtuous circle is completed through the highly competitive manufacturing prices that Octopus's scale of operations enable it to obtain.

In May 1981, Octopus mounted what constituted, though not conceived in those terms, a direct challenge to paperbacks with the establishment of Bounty Books. This was done in conjunction with Websters Group, significantly best known for its subsidiary Bookwise, which is the dominant force in the distribution of paperbacks in the UK. Bounty Books can be said to occupy a position at the top end of the hardback bargain book market. The books are reissues of earlier titles from Octopus and other sources, sold at very advantageous prices, with the original price being clearly indicated on the covers together with the Bounty Book price which may well be half that of the original. The choice of titles is Bookwise's, who select the titles after consultation with Octopus; all titles are exclusive to Bookwise who buy firm from Octopus and sell firm to retail outlets. Production is the responsibility of Octopus. In the first eight months of operation in 1981, turnover amounted to £1m; in 1982 it came close to £2.2m and the current annual rate is probably in excess of £4m.

Octopus is not alone among hardback houses in aiming to win back the reader who has defected to paperbacks for reasons of economy. The October 1983 launch by William Heinemann of a new hardback imprint, Landmark, made available to the book buyer at £4.95 such titles as D. H. Lawrence's Sons and Lovers, Graham Greene's Brighton Rock and Harper Lee's To Kill a Mockingbird. At that price, many a trade paperback selling at £2.95, £3.95, or more, no longer looks given away.

Further encouragement for the cause of hardbacks comes from the USA, where there is ample evidence of a narrowing in the price gap between hardbacks and paperbacks other than mass-market, currently leading to a shift of purchases towards the former. A Gallup survey of book buying in November and December, 1983 indicated that whereas 31 per cent of hardback books purchased were sold at less than their cover price, the proportion of paperbacks was 18 per cent. In another analysis, the cover prices of trade paperbacks published by some 24 US houses rose 22 per cent in 1982, after a more than 30 per cent rise the previous year. One factor contributing to this trend has been the dramatic growth of book chains such as Waldenbooks and B. Dalton which has provided a rising number of towns with their first bookshops, thereby putting within the reach of the customer a choice of best-selling hardcover books. As John P. Dessauer comments 'at a time when the bargain appeal of hardcovers is at its height, what with extensive remaindering, reprinting and discounting, the overpriced paperback of weak appeal is at a cruel disadvantage'[1].

[1] Publishers Weekly, January 13, 1984

PRODUCTION

Traditionally, British publishers bought the great bulk of their book production requirements within the UK - almost as a matter of course.

The incentives for change on the part of publishers were for the most part lacking. In the period 1950-65 for example, UK book publishing experienced significant and consistent growth, with industry turnover rising at a compound rate of some 7.25 per cent; within that total, exports expanded at an above-average rate of 9.75 per cent and home sales at 5.75 per cent. Over the same period, book prices rose at slightly less than 6 per cent, indicating an annual rate of growth in real terms of perhaps 1.25 per cent to 1.5 per cent. Not earth shattering, perhaps, but comfortable. Furthermore, the greater buoyancy of exports was underwritten as it were, by a substantial decline in the value of sterling over the period, which ensured that domestic UK inflation, often at a rate in excess of that occurring in overseas countries, did not damage the price competitiveness of British books in foreign markets.

Within the UK itself, competition between printers tended to be in terms of service rather than price; this encouraged fidelity/immobility in the relationships between individual publishers and individual printers. It was traditional for UK printers to raise their prices once a year, following the annual spring wage negotiations with the production unions. Up to 1956, the size of the increase was the result of consultation among the printers. In that year, however, this practice ceased, which meant that increases were the product of publishers looking over their respective shoulders at their rivals. While this meant a greater variation in prices charged than was previously the case, it was still true that prices tended to be bunched and that printers established their individual prices by reference to UK cost rises and UK trading conditions in which they all shared.

Then sterling came to be recognized as a petro-currency and appreciated against the basket of currencies by 9.75 per cent in 1979, and by 13 per cent in 1980. At the same time, UK costs continued to accelerate, with printing wage increases in 1979 and 1980 averaging 15 per cent and 20 per cent respectively. This rapidly meant that in many UK publishers' export markets, UK-produced books ended up by being at least 25 per cent more expensive than, say, US-produced books. Hence, the absolute necessity for UK publishers who wished to protect their positions overseas to buy their print overseas.

Overseas Buying

The practice of going overseas for book manufacturing had started well before 1979 for a number of UK companies, chiefly the larger firms. The nationwide strike of printing unions in 1959, which was followed by a big (for those days) 4½ per cent wage increase, had stimulated Longmans, for example, to establish close links with a Hong Kong printer. The fact that 70 per cent of Longman's sales were made overseas was an additional reason for their trying to protect themselves from the hazards of UK industrial relations. Octopus Books is another instance of a UK publisher which, from an early stage, has relied heavily on overseas manufacturing: in 1979 'well over half' of Octopus's print bill already went abroad. Once again, special considerations may be cited, notably Octopus's involvement in international co-editions and the emphasis on colour in its books, where overseas printers have long enjoyed a strong position.

The really significant development, however, has been the widespread use in the last few years of overseas manufacturing by UK publishers, the results of which have been seen in a reduction since 1980 of 30 per cent in numbers employed in UK book production, and by the total disappearance, or major eclipse, of such names as Morrison & Gibb, Oxley Printing, C. H. Nichols, Hunt Barnard and Fakenham Press.

The truth of the matter is that book production has now become an international business, supplying goods and services to UK publishing, an industry which itself has always been international. In a comment in Printing World[1], Anthony Rowe, Managing Director of The Pitman Press, summarizes the position of British book printers:

'A UK book printer who tries, Canute-like, to get publishers to pay him prices based on his costs plus a margin, regardless of whether his costs and resulting prices are world-competitive, is cutting his own throat. What he has to do is to cut his costs so that the world price gives him the margin needed to make enough profit for investment. And that is likely to be the most difficult thing he has ever to do.'

For UK publishers this internationalization of book manufacturing presents a challenge - how to get the best terms, consistent with maintenance of quality and service - as well as opportunity - how best to control what amounts to the single most important variable cost that a publisher has to bear. A cost, moreover, which traditionally has supported the structure of book pricing and hence the economics of book publishing.

The Australian Experience

In terms of opportunities, the history of Australian publishing provides an extreme, but nonetheless interesting, example. It was in 1963 that Lansdowne Press became the first Australian

[1] Printing World, September 22, 1982

publisher to print in Asia. This initial experience in fact proved unfortunate, but nonetheless started a trend which has resulted in up to three-quarters of Australian hardback titles now being produced in Hong Kong, Singapore and Japan. In the opinion of Lloyd O'Neil, the founder of Lansdowne Press, by freeing the Australian book from the limitations of Australian printing costs, this enabled it to become competitive with the imported book. It is also worth pointing to the fact that, with Australian publishing serving a numerically small domestic market, the competitiveness of Asian printing was not based on long runs. Writing on the subject of children's publishing in Australia, Walter McVitty of Melbourne State College has confirmed that this remains the case: 'Through going to cost-cutting Asian printers Australian publishers have managed to produce picture books which are artistically and technically outstanding, yet priced substantially lower than large run UK imports'. Furthermore, it is interesting to note that Australian publishers were finding Hong Kong, Japanese and Singapore printers satisfactory on the grounds of quality and service at a time when most UK publishers would have expressed grave reservations.

International Comparisons

Turning to opportunities available to UK publishers, the 1981 _Printing World_ Book Production Supplement carried a table showing various international quotations for the printing and binding of a large (496 page) colour encyclopaedia, in a run of 50,000 copies, and including 500 illustrations of which 250 were in colour. The prices per copy quoted in the following table are all ex works and relate to identical manufacturing specifications. No allowance is made, however, for the extra shipping time (some three weeks) required from the Far East compared to continental Europe.

The book in question was placed in Spain, where the winning quote of £1.83 was 24 per cent below the lowest UK quote, and 34 per cent below the highest UK quote. Furthermore, the most competitive UK price was higher than any of the other prices. A UK publisher who failed under these circumstances to investigate overseas manufacturing possibilities, would have done himself a considerable disservice. Undoubtedly, currency swings explain a significant proportion of such price differentials, which are consequently subject to considerable change over periods that may be quite short. Clearly, also, the example quoted is of a book with special characteristics. The essential point, however, is that the UK publisher should have the freedom of manoeuvre and the practical knowledge to take advantage of such situations as they arise. Nor are pricing opportunities of this kind confined to highly priced books. In 1980 Picture Puffins were being printed in the Far East for savings of up to 25 per cent. While in the whole area of typesetting, similar economies were being achieved in India, the Far East and to a lesser extent in the USA. Complex typesetting in the UK was not, however, subject to the same competitive pressures.

Table 64

Quotations on a One-Volume Colour Encyclopaedia

Hong Kong	£1.89	£1.98	£2.23
Singapore	£1.93	£2.03	£2.04
UK	£2.40	£2.43	£2.66	£2.78
USA	£2.19	£2.30		
Spain	£1.83	£1.86	£1.95
Italy	£2.14	£2.14	£2.37
Belgium	£2.08		
Holland	£2.18		

Source: Book Production Supplement, Printing World March 4, 1981.

This is by no means to say that UK production has a minor role to play. Blackwell Press's typical Bookplan products (novels of 192 pages with a run of 5,000) have remained price competitive throughout the worst periods of sterling strength. Ladybird Books provides a remarkable example of the fusion of efficient production and publishing. The economics of printing black and white in the UK have improved markedly with the more recent currency swings. Greater emphasis on shorter runs, allied to reductions in stocks at the wholesale and retail levels, have served to enhance the importance of rapid delivery, where the UK industry has a clear geographical edge. More generally, many UK printers have greatly increased their ability to compete by cutting out uneconomic activities, reducing the numbers of those employed in the areas retained and spending substantially on modern equipment. And the downward trend of sterling has helped to restore the international competitiveness of UK book manufacturing. But this emphatically does not mean that the UK publisher need now look no further than East Anglia for his production: the titles in Heinemann's Landmark imprint, launched in January 1984, are being produced in Finland, for example, on straight grounds of price.

Trends in Production

In considering the outlook for British book publishers, the trends in production are of considerable importance. If the experience of the USA proves to be a guide to likely developments in other countries, the use of word processors seems certain to expand dramatically. In the USA it is increasingly common for authors to be supplied with word processors by their book publishers. But where the author submits his book in the traditional typescript, it can now make economic sense for the publisher to have the text retyped on a word processor so that all the editing may be done on the visual display screen. This is indeed the case with the present report. The cassette (or diskette), whether it comes directly from the author or from the publisher's word processing unit, is then sent to the typesetter for the tape of 'idiot key strokes' (which describes the state of the tape at that stage) to be programmed and processed. The publisher has merely supplied the author's words and punctuation on cassette. The 'justification', hyphenation, choice of typefaces and transformation into page proofs on computerized photo composition equipment are the province of the typesetter.

There are instances of publishers who not only equip themselves with word processors, but also undertake the typesetting stage themselves. To many, however, this would seem to lead to an undesirable element of vertical integration. It involves the publisher in tying up capital, directly or indirectly, in expensive equipment, which is subject to obsolescence. And where that occurs, it denies to the publishing arm access to the most up-to-date equipment which is available in the market place.

At the machining and binding stage one area of technological development is aimed at meeting publishers' growing needs (noted earlier) for short runs at short notice. Modern computerized web offset presses, for example, make runs of as little as 10,000 copies an economic proposition, thanks in part to a drastic reduction in wastage from as much as 25 per cent to 10 per cent or lower. A publisher whose vertical integration takes him into printing and binding is once again in a position of either committing considerable resources so as to remain fully competitive, or denying the publishing side advantages it might otherwise obtain.

In recent years, we have seen swings in currencies create great opportunities for publishers whose print buying is flexible and who have organized themselves to take full advantage of such flexibility. At the same time, publishers lacking this freedom of international manoeuvre through commitment to domestic production have been severely penalized.

Within the UK, fiercely competitive conditions have forced UK printers greatly to improve the efficiency of their operations, often based on a combination of reductions in labour and expenditure on capital. The expansion in demand for books produced in short runs for swift delivery is opening up a market somewhat freer from international competition, for which certain UK printers are specifically equipping themselves. Once again the print buyer who has the freedom of manoeuvre and who has organized himself so as to be able to profit from this freedom, enjoys a valuable competitive advantage over rival publishers lacking these characteristics.

It is sometimes argued that book production, which is now clearly in a buyer's market, could swing back to a seller's market, partly as a result of the sharp reduction in capacity arising out of the rationalization of the British industry. Once demand picks up, it is suggested that those publishers who have their captive manufacturing interests will once again enjoy the advantages of vertical integration. While undoubtedly there will be variations in the extent to which the edge is with the buyer (or the seller), there has been a fundamental change that suggests the impossibility of a full return to the earlier situation: namely recognition by UK publishers that book production is international in scope. In addition, there is the point noted earlier that technological change has removed much of the craft limitations affecting book production, with the result that there is much greater freedom of entry into the industry than before. All of this is likely to put a brake on any movement from surplus to shortage in book manufacturing capacity. The evidence points to the conclusion that where a printer owns a publisher this remains a cause for celebration, but where a publisher owns a printer the prospective advantages continue to be extremely dubious.

THE AMERICAN CHALLENGE

In the 10 years from 1972 to 1982 US book exports in value terms have expanded steadily from $172m to $641m, an increase of 273 per cent or 14.1 per cent per annum. Adjusted for inflation (the Consumer Price Index) the rise has been of the order of 62 per cent or 4.9 per cent per annum. This compares with UK book exports advancing from £101m in 1972 to £336m in 1982, an increase of 233 per cent or 12.8 per cent per annum. But in real terms (adjusting for the Retail Price Index) this amounts to an actual reduction of 11 per cent, or one per cent per annum. Taken at face value these figures undoubtedly suggest that the US book publishing industry relative to the UK book publishing industry has been gaining market share in countries outside the USA.

Table 65

US Book Exports

($million)	1972	1975	1977	1978	1979
TOTAL	172.12	269.36	314.16	370.62	439.25
Bibles (a)	8.25	13.32	18.39	20.73	23.94
Dictionaries (b)	2.87	4.45	6.12	3.97	5.74
Encyclopaedias	24.40	31.91	24.59	32.29	29.88
Textbooks	40.56	63.90	72.06	70.30	83.55
Technical (c)	30.16	43.96	45.30	49.48	51.58
Other	61.53	105.50	142.40	187.45	237.89
Picture Books (d)	4.35	6.32	5.30	6.40	6.67

($million)	1980	1981	1982	Nine months 1982	1983
TOTAL	511.62	603.20	641.36	491.89	453.08
Bibles (a)	31.87	33.90	31.87	23.84	23.52
Dictionaries (b)	6.02	7.10	5.75	5.01	5.07
Encyclodaedias	27.95	25.82	25.35	20.90	21.88
Textbooks	99.66	118.72	130.79	102.92	81.00
Technical (c)	53.93	79.64	118.49	88.16	92.13
Other	284.14	327.17	319.66	244.07	223.18
Picture Books (d)	8.05	10.85	9.45	6.99	6.30

(a) Includes testaments. (b) Includes thesauruses
(c) Includes scientific books. (d) Includes picture and colouring books
Source: US Commerce Department

125

The subject categories into which US exports are divided are shown in Table 65. It should be pointed out that US export statistics currently exclude export shipments having a value of less than $500 and to that extent are understated; up to 1979, the exclusion related to shipments having a value of $250, leading to a degree of non-comparability within these statistics.

Easily the fastest growth has been achieved by the residual 'other' category, followed by technical and scientific books and bibles and testaments. Textbook sales and children's picture book sales have risen more rapidly than those of dictionaries. The major laggard has been exports of encyclopaedias whose sales by value are barely up over the 10-year period, having achieved a peak in 1978, from which they have declined by 21 per cent.

Table 66

Percentage Changes in US Book Exports by Category

(per cent)	1972 to 1982 TOTAL	1972 to 1977	1977 to 1982 Annual rates	1972 to 1982
TOTAL	+273	+12.8	+15.3	+14.1
Bibles etc	+286	+17.4	+11.6	+14.5
Dictionaries	+100	+16.4	-1.3	+7.2
Encyclopaedias	+4	+0.1	+0.4	+0.4
Textbooks	+122	+12.2	+12.7	+12.4
Technical etc	+293	+8.5	+21.2	+14.7
Other	+420	+18.3	+17.6	+17.9
Picture books	+117	+4.0	+12.3	+8.1

Source: US Commerce Department

One of the difficulties of the figures covering the two five-year periods is that they hinge on 1977 which was a year when one series was exceptionally buoyant, namely dictionaries and thesauruses, and another, encyclopaedias, was depressed. If one ignores those two classes of books, it is interesting to note the deceleration in bibles and testaments and the acceleration in technical and scientific books (influenced by a considerable jump in 1982) and in picture books. Steady growth has been achieved by textbooks. But it is in the very important 'other' category that exports have advanced most rapidly over the two periods.

Looking at the very recent experience, there is evidence of a distinct slowing down in US book exports, with the advance in 1982 amounting to only 6 per cent - against a ten-year average of 14.1 per cent - while in the first nine months of 1983 there was an actual drop of 7.9 per cent against a year earlier. This pattern coincides neatly with a rise in the dollar and with a severe worldwide recession. If one takes Nigeria out of the calculations, the drop comes out at 5.8 per cent for the first nine months of 1983.

A geographical analysis of US book exports highlights the main foreign markets for the US book trade, as well as the wide variations in the rates of change over the last ten years.

Table 67

US Book Exports to Selected Countries

($million)	1972	1975	1977	1978	1979
TOTAL	172.12	269.36	314.16	370.62	439.25
UK	20.92	34.25	32.92	44.25	63.72
Canada	83.25	118.56	148.99	147.60	170.12
Australia	13.83	27.94	27.56	36.71	40.69
New Zealand	1.82	2.54	2.38	4.13	6.65
Japan	10.02	14.30	15.44	23.19	21.56
Nigeria	0.21	0.78	1.35	2.02	2.60
India	1.64	2.62	4.91	6.23	5.95
South Africa	2.91	4.20	3.10	4.10	4.38
Holland	4.38	7.97	9.64	10.01	9.66
W. Germany	2.94	3.74	3.65	5.15	7.92
All other	30.20	52.45	64.21	87.23	106.01

				Nine months	
($million)	1980	1981	1982	1982	1983
TOTAL	511.62	603.20	641.36	491.89	453.08
UK	94.26	90.11	82.57	63.14	64.59
Canada	191.30	221.49	237.70	182.87	176.56
Australia	39.02	53.35	57.03	44.59	39.89
New Zealand	6.75	7.77	8.21	6.64	4.46
Japan	20.30	21.31	24.84	18.81	18.88
Nigeria	9.56	22.12	21.19	18.93	7.56
India	4.34	4.87	6.18	4.84	4.95
South Africa	6.04	10.57	12.25	9.13	6.74
Holland	11.10	14.65	17.29	12.03	17.29
W. Germany	8.46	9.61	11.84	8.60	8.17
All other	120.49	147.35	162.26	122.31	103.99

Source: US Commerce Department

While it is undoubtedly true that rates of growth can be distorted by erratic movements from one year to another, on the whole the pattern has been fairly consistent both for broad subject sectors and individual countries.

A feature of Table 68 is the comparatively modest advance of US exports to Canada, which is far and away the single most important market for US books: over the period covered, the rise of 186 per cent compares with one of 273 per cent for total book exports and this has resulted in Canada's share of total US book exports falling from 48.4 per cent in 1972 to 37.1 per cent in 1982. Table 68 furthermore reveals a slowing down in the rate of export growth. Within the subject breakdown for Canada, sales growth was comparatively sluggish in encyclopaedias (+19 per cent over the full ten years) and technical and scientific books (+52 per cent). The modesty of US export growth in the technical and scientific classification may mask a more active local publishing programme by Canadian subsidiaries of US publishing houses. Areas of above-average growth have been the residual 'other' category (+295 per cent) and bibles (+288 per cent).

Table 68

Percentage Changes in US Exports to Selected Countries

(per cent)	1972 to 1982 TOTAL	1972 to 1977	1977 to 1982	1972 to 1982
			Annual rates	
TOTAL	+273	+12.8	+15.3	+14.1
UK	+295	+9.5	+20.2	+14.7
Canada	+186	+12.3	+9.8	+11.1
Australia	+312	+14.8	+15.6	+15.2
New Zealand	+351	+5.5	+28.0	+16.3
Japan	+148	+9.0	+10.0	+9.5
Nigeria	+914	+45.0	+73.5	+58.9
India	+277	+24.5	+4.7	+14.2
South Africa	+321	+1.3	+31.6	+15.5
Holland	+295	+17.1	+12.4	+14.7
West Germany	+303	+4.4	+26.5	+15.0
All other	+437	+16.3	+20.3	+18.2

In the United Kingdom which now absorbs 12.9 per cent of US exports compared to 12.1 per cent in 1972, US sales have accelerated sharply in the latest five-year period. Of the $62m increase in exports over the full ten years, $43m occurred in the residual 'other' category, which expanded from $5m in 1972 to $48m in 1982; the latter total was down from a peak of $68.4m in 1980. No assessment is possible of the importance of re-exports where for example a US publisher uses its UK company as a staging post for its sales to say the Continent or the Middle East or Africa. What seems fairly certain, though, is that the explosion that occurred in 1978, 1979 and 1980 was in part linked to the dramatic rise of sterling vis-à-vis the dollar: the exchange rate went from an average of $1.78 to the £ in 1977, to $1.93 in 1978, to $2.16 in 1979, and to $2.33 in 1980. This induced some UK publishers to shift some of their manufacturing to the USA from the UK, leading to a boost in US exports to the UK representing that part of the print run of a UK publisher's title that was destined for the UK market. More generally, sales of US published books distributed in the UK by agents or subsidiaries were enhanced by their increased price competitiveness. And finally, the high price of sterling was a powerful incentive for UK remainder companies to buy their product in the USA, quite often with little reference to where the UK rights were held.

Table 69

US Book Exports to the UK by Subject Classification

($thousand)	1980	1981	1982	Nine months 1982	1983
TOTAL	94,264	90,108	82,570	63,135	64,592
Bibles	2,005	2,085	3,025	2,255	2,056
Dictionaries	1,826	619	802	638	2,150
Encyclopaedias	2,116	2,472	2,584	1,787	1,494
Textbooks	13,480	12,820	9,759	7,520	9,817
Technical & scient.	6,238	11,574	17,983	14,325	13,927
Other	68,383	59,867	48,126	36,610	35,148
Picture books	216	671	291	-	-

The year 1981 saw a sharp reversal in these trends in the foreign exchange market, with the dollar rising smartly against sterling. The exchange rate went from $2.39 at the close of 1980 to $1.91 at the end of 1981; at December 1982 it stood at $1.62 and by the end of September, 1983 at $1.50. The category analysis of US exports to the UK shows textbooks and 'other' responsive to these influences, while technical and scientific books appear to have ignored them. The most recent period has somewhat surprisingly shown some modest overall growth, in contrast to the general trend of US exports. On analysis, the buoyancy is limited to textbooks and encyclopaedias, while all the other sectors are down on a year earlier.

Looking at some of the other countries, 15 per cent growth has been roughly achieved over the full period in such markets as Australia, India, South Africa, Holland and New Zealand. Above-average growth growth has characterized US exports to Nigeria and the residual 'other' category. Exports to Japan have been well below average. Within the ten years covered, there has been a sharp acceleration in US exports to New Zealand, South Africa, West Germany and 'other', while the rate of expansion in sales to India has fallen away.

In terms of subject, Australia and South Africa have been steadily expanding markets for US exports of bibles and testaments. US textbook sales have risen substantially to Australia, Japan and South Africa. Exports of technical and scientific books have grown markedly to West Germany, the Netherlands and Japan. In all countries the 'other' category has shown above-average growth, being in particular very largely responsible for the sharp jumps in overall exports in 1981. Such residual figures certainly reflect a multitude of influences, including:

(a) the export of US remainders which achieved 'dumping' characteristics in some markets in 1980 and 1981;

(b) the undercutting of UK titles (paperbacks being a case in point), as a result of differing rates of inflation and movements in the exchange rate;

(c) more successful marketing of US exports.

The delayed impact of the Nigerian economic difficulties is reflected in a collapse of US exports in the first nine months of 1983 to $7.56m from $18.93m in the same period a year earlier.

Throughout, the analysis has been concentrated on value figures. In unit terms, the performance of US exports has been very much more muted. This is emphasized in a study prepared by the late Curtis Benjamin, former chairman and president of McGraw Hill who pointed out that the prices of the books making up most of US exports came close to doubling between 1974 and 1980: a 77 per cent rise in total export sales by value was virtually cancelled by inflation, with the result that unit sales expanded by less than one per cent over the six year period[1]. This means that the export figures given at the start of this section which are adjusted for inflation using the Consumer Price Index overstate the amount of real growth in US book exports. It is possible, therefore, that the opening comment of this chapter suggesting that US publishers have been increasing market share relative to UK book publishers needs to be shaded.

1. The Experience of Selected US Publishing Houses

Following the presentation of statistics for the industry as a whole, it may be of some use to look at certain case histories

[1] 'US Book Sales Overseas: An Ebbing Tide' by Curtis Benjamin. Publishers Weekly, April 29, 1983

of US publishers. One thought is that this could help to
illustrate not only the challenges but also some of the opportunities that US firms' differing approaches to foreign markets
can offer to UK houses.

The alternatives open to US poublishers in respect of foreign
sales are the same as those open to UK publishers. The main
contrasts between one country and the other lie in the absolute
figures and the percentages involved.

As noted earlier, the international aspect of US publishing
has typically been very much less marked than has been the case
in the United Kingdom. This is explained by a whole variety of
influences, most important of which has been the sheer size of
the domestic market and the fact, therefore, that it has been
possible for publishers to have a very comfortable existence
supplying US needs without reference to foreign sales. Another
factor which is perhaps given rather less weight than ought to
be the case is the personal one of the temperamental
'insularity' of the majority of Americans. The strength of the
movement in the Second World War of isolation finds its counterpart at the commercial level.

The war did, however, push many US industries into supplying
the needs of foreign countries which had previously been
satisfied from European sources and this was also true of the
aftermath, when acute shortages persisted. In publishing, one
may date the build-up of US involvement in the export of educational texts at the tertiary level from this period. It is also
sometimes forgotten that certain countries such as Australia
and New Zealand imposed selective import restrictions: up to
1959, it was extremely difficult to import into Australia fiction and bibles (a somewhat improbable combination) and this
deflected the efforts of US publishers into other areas,
notably tertiary texts.

2. Trade Publishing

Trade publishing is the area where the international flavour of
US publishing is at its weakest. This is epitomized by Simon &
Schuster, second in size to Random House among trade publishing
houses in the USA. Out of total sales of some $200 million,
exports amount to about 5 per cent and rights income to
approximately 4 per cent. Company policy is to secure wherever
possible world English language rights and, subsequently, to
trade these rights. The company no longer has any foreign
operations of its own, having had to divest itself of its
Canadian subsidiary following the acquisition in 1975 of Simon &
Schuster by the conglomerate Gulf & Western.

As the president, Richard Snyder, expresses it, Simon &
Schuster is a US house and he is very reluctant to see top
management efforts dissipated in running overseas operations,
with the concomitant demands on executive time (much of it

travel) and skill. Furthermore, he himself recognizes that he is not temperamentally an internationalist, and that he regards his main concern, and that of his senior colleagues, as being the development of the US business. Since he is a staunch believer in the merits of size, this also dovetails with an emphasis on the domestic market.

Such an approach does not, however, preclude Simon & Schuster from seeking to improve on its overseas business. The $8m of rights income was only $2m some five years ago; this is admittedly in part a reflection of management's policy of securing world English language rights - and is therefore to a significant extent offset by the advances to authors made in that connection - but it does illustrate a more aggressive approach to the foreign aspects of trade publishing.

Silhouette

Simon & Schuster's solution to the international marketing of its paperback romance imprint, Silhouette, is particularly interesting. On the one hand it illustrates how a US firm gets effective overseas exposure with a minimum of financial and managerial commitment and on the other hand it shows how a UK firm manages to profit from what amounts otherwise to US encroachment into UK traditional markets.

The background to the creation of the Silhouette imprint is worth sketching. Simon & Schuster previously undertook the distribution of Harlequin titles in the USA. Somewhat more than three and a half years ago Mills & Boon made the decision to do their own distribution and withdrew the agency from Simon & Schuster. Having, as it were, learned the business, Simon & Schuster themselves decided to move aggressively into the romance market with their own imprint, which was launched in the USA three and a quarter years ago. It then made commercial sense for Simon & Schuster to spread the costs of development as widely as posssible and this led, six months later, to the selection of Hodder & Stoughton as overseas partners under what amounts to a form of franchise agreement.

Hodder & Stoughton control the traditional British market rights for the full range of Silhouette titles, all the editorial costs of which are borne by Simon & Schuster. Hodder & Stoughton purchase the film from Simon & Schuster and have the use of the American jackets. For their part, Hodder & Stoughton are responsible for production - the costs of which are kept low through there being no composition - warehousing, distribution and, most important of all, promotion. The scale of the promotion costs is illustrated in the fact that in a five-month period (August to December 1982) Silhouette spent £125,000 in women's UK magazines; it also announced a £100,000 advertising campaign on Scottish TV. Mills & Boon's total UK promotional expenditure over two years to the end of 1982 is put at £2.5m. The sums are largely explained by the fact that romance publishers are marketing brand names, not individual titles.

Scale of operations (ie depth of publishing) is clearly of crucial importance, hence the proliferation of secondary series created by Simon & Schuster. In addition to Romances, they have launched Special Edition and Desire, both romance series but with more developed plotting and a rather more modern approach. They also publish First Love, a series of young adult (teenage) romances. Much of the selling in the UK is through Bookwise's paperback distribution division whose penetration both to CTNs (confectionery, tobacco and newsagent shops) and to chains such as Woolworths, Boots and Martins, is a perfect fit for the market for which the titles are destined.

Another essential ingredient in romance fiction publishing is a military-type precision in publishing - say, six titles a month, with runs of 100,000 plus, appearing on a specific day, priced at 75 pence each, 192 pages long and in covers that are clearly identified with the series in question.

Hodder & Stoughton operate the licence for Australia, in such a way that their subsidiary has the same form of relationship with the parent as the latter has with Simon & Schuster.

The terms of payment by Hodder & Stoughton are obviously not public, but the basis consists of advances on UK and British market sales which include a significant premium over and above the amounts that Simon & Schuster (and the authors) would normally receive. After such advances have been earned, additional royalties are paid.

In reviewing this joint venture, some of the points that strike an outsider are as follows:

(a) The UK publisher has capitalized on his long-established position in the UK and traditional British markets.

(b) The UK publisher has capitalized, furthermore, on his established position in paperback publishing.

(c) The UK publisher is using more intensively his existing warehousing and distribution systems.

(d) The UK publisher is expanding his existing business through a new activity that requires little in the way of increased personnel. Senior executives are, however, heavily involved.

(e) One of the most important contributions made by the UK publisher consists of capital in the form of advances (normal in most kinds of publishing) and a heavy promotional budget (special to romance publishing).

(f) To achieve success, the UK publisher clearly has to make a heavy commitment in terms of effort (apart from capital) which leaves no room for half measures, or an attitude that regards the venture as a sideline.

Feffer and Simons

As a further illustration of the role played by foreign sales in US publishing, the operations of Feffer and Simons, the

Doubleday subsidiary, are of considerable interest. One of the major activities of Feffer and Simons is the representation of an impressive total of some 200 American publishing firms in all or part of their foreign markets. Feffer and Simons' role is threefold. Firstly in selling, secondly in service and thirdly in finance.

On the selling side, they act as a postbox for their clients' catalogues and undertake to distribute them to the appropriate foreign outlets. In addition, they themselves cannibalize such catalogues to create specialist lists which they send out on their relevant mailing lists. This work is done by three marketing divisions covering:

(a) trade (books mainly sold through bookshops);
(b) education (primarily at the tertiary level); and
(c) mass market (which includes both mass-market paperbacks and magazines).

These marketing divisions in turn break down their operations between nine marketing regions which are the responsibility of area regional sales managers answering to the three divisional marketing managers.

The bulk of Feffer and Simons' book business consists of selling on indent, in response to orders received from around the world, many arising out of the catalogues that they distribute. Normally, the books are then shipped from the publishers' own warehouses. However, Feffer and Simons do themselves operate a number of warehouses overseas, notably in Holland (whose catchment area is the continent of Europe), England, India, Japan (in conjunction with a Japanese partner), the Philippines, Mexico and Australia. Feffer and Simons limit the choice of titles that they stock to the faster movers (sales of at least 4,000 units a year). Stocks represent firm purchases but return privileges are often granted, within certain constraints, by individual publishers. In general terms, the company follows a cautious policy, and relies for much of its business on preselling.

In the areas of service and finance, Feffer and Simons can be said to take the fuss out of exporting. Their customers get monthly statements and are paid in US dollars within thirty days, while the foreign outlet receives the normal discount. The US publishers, therefore, avoid any problems of doubtful receivables - an important consideration in view of the international nature of the business - do not have to cope themselves with the financial side and obtain payment promptly. In addition, they pass on to a specialist the sales task, and all the complexities and organizational and financial complications that that implies. In return they pay over to Feffer and Simons 8 per cent of the retail value of the books sold (or around 15 per cent of their net receipts).

As an indication of scale, Feffer and Simons' total sales are running at around $70m, of which some 60 per cent or $42m is accounted for by books and 40 per cent or $28m by magazines.

134

Their total staff is around 130, of which 30 are in sales and marketing and 100 in accounts and administration. Profits 'normally' fall within the $1.2m to $1.4m range. In recent years the company has experienced a somewhat static sales and profits pattern after a period of significant growth. This can be explained by some falling away of export business, which in most recent times has been associated with the depressing effects on sales that a rising dollar undoubtedly has, since the overseas customer is charged the US retail price (less the normal discount). Another explanation, which points in exactly the opposite direction, lies in the danger to Feffer and Simons that success on their part alerts clients to the scope that exists in foreign markets, and encourages them to withdraw part or all of their export business from Feffer and Simons with a view to other more exclusive arrangements, or their undertaking the task themselves. The truth of the matter appears to lie between the two explanations.

For UK publishers, the Feffer and Simons example illustrates in the first instance the willingness of hundreds of US publishers to share a common export channel. However efficient such a channel may be, it does suggest that direct exports must be relatively modest for such publishers and that they are treated as marginal in relation to the individual firms' business as a whole. The more recent trends cannot, however, be any real reason for complacency on the part of UK publishers: an improvement in the competitive position of non-US books, thanks to a foreign exchange movement, provides uncertain protection for, as we know very well from our own experience, massive swings can occur in the foreign exchange markets over relatively short periods of time. In addition, the actions of those publishers who have chosen to organize their export business differently at the very least points to a less laissez faire attitude. Working in the other direction, one should not underestimate the sense of exasperation that US businessmen - often not at home in international trading - experience when faced with the vagaries of exchange rates: the strength of the US dollar has in the short term undoubtedly contributed to a dismissive attitude to overseas business by some US publishers and the 1983 Mexican devaluation may well have sharpened this to four-letter hostility.

Other US Publishers

If one is still allowed to treat Bantam as a US publisher, despite acquisition of control by Bertelsmann in 1977, this is one US firm in the mass-market area whose stated goals remain explicitly international.

At the start of 1981, Transworld Australia was set up with the task of taking over from Gordon & Gotch the distribution of both Bantam and Corgi titles in Australia. In addition, the

135

longer term goal of developing indigenous publishing was acknowledged with the appointment of a consultant editor. In 1982 a minority interest was acquired in a major South African wholesale distributor, Superbooks. The size of the interest is believed to be of the order of 25 per cent. Superbooks has replaced a small sales unit that Corgi previously had in South Africa and has become the sole distributor in South Africa of both Bantam and Corgi titles (outside of the Central News Agency chain which continues to buy direct). Superbooks' distribution arrangements for other UK publishers such as Penguin and Octopus have so far remained unchanged. In another move affecting, this time, Bantam's Canadian operations, since April 1983 Bantam's Canadian subsidiary has been distributing Corgi titles, thereby taking over from Penguin.

This activity in Bantam's overseas interests is clearly aimed at increasing their sales strengths for the benefit of both Bantam and Corgi. One intriguing aspect to this is that while Bantam has frequently stated that it does not accept the British spheres of influence in the pattern of international book distribution, the Australian company is a subsidiary of the UK subsidiary, not the US parent, and the interest in the South African company is held through Corgi, not Bantam, with Corgi's chief executive Paul Scherer on the board. Traditional British trading links still seem to possess some redeeming features.

Times Mirror, on the other hand, is an example of a publisher that has been going in the other direction, specifically reducing its direct foreign exposure in the mass-market field through its sale in May 1981 of its paperback company, New English Library, to Hodder & Stoughton; this involved Times Mirror in a US$2m write-off. Management's view was that NEL, which at the time of its sale was believed to be trading close to break-even, was highly marginal to the Group's overall interests and fairly demanding in terms of management effort. No sustained attempt had been made to develop an indigenous publishing activity, with top management unwilling to invest the time and money required for the establishment of local publishing units.

This approach applies to all of Times Mirror's book publishing interests, with foreign sales being achieved through exports, preferably via exclusive distributors, who are responsible for sales and promotion. Australia provides an example of the arrangements made by Times Mirror in a significant overseas market. The agency for Harry N. Abrams, publisher of art and fine illustrated books is held by Macmillans Australia, the paperback imprint Signet is carried by Collins, the legal publisher Matthew Bender by Associated Book Publishers' subsidiary the Law Book Company and the nursing/medical publishers C. V. Mosby, by Ramsay Surgical. The overseas agent acquires the book on a 50 per cent discount on the US $ cover price in the case of most hardback titles, but bears all the transportation costs. Credit is granted in respect of returns on the basis of stripped covers (inspected by a Times Mirror representative) and the return of the title pages in respect of professional books.

Times Mirror provides an example of a US group that is large enough to organize separate distribution arrangements, rather than join the 200-odd firms that go to Feffer and Simons. Foreign sales, nonetheless, remain marginal to its business, being described as 'the icing on the cake' and 'not at all critical'.

3. **Professional Titles**

Professional titles, which for these purposes include tertiary texts, represent the area of US publishing that has the longest and the most firmly rooted tradition of foreign sales. Indeed, as we have noted earlier, the dislocation of the war, and of the immediate post-war years, acted as a particularly strong influence on US publishers of professional titles in introducing them to export markets.

Gordon Graham, Chairman of Butterworths and previously head of McGraw-Hill UK, in a speech to the technical, scientific and medical group of the American Publishers Association in March 1979 estimated that between 1950 and 1970 the British publishing trade had lost about half of its technical/scientific/medical export markets. In traditional British outlets such as India, Pakistan, Malaysia and Australia, American books secured about half of the market, starting from an insignificant base. In countries such as Japan, Indonesia and the Philippines, where the British presence was much less evident, American publications predominate. Another statistic that dovetails with the first is his calculation that between 1958 and 1972 about forty US academic and scholarly publishers started subsidiaries in Britain alone.

The post-war history of McGraw-Hill's book publishing interests is a good example of how US publishers of educational and professional books developed their foreign side. Initially, McGraw-Hill's foreign operations consisted of exports from the USA to overseas customers. Export sales of leading US scientific and technical book publishers accounted for only 5-6 per cent of sales before the Second World War. This compared with 40 per cent of sales for the UK book publishing industry, and as much as 60 per cent for German publishers, who were particularly strong in science and technology. The export sales of Spanish publishers reached as high as 60 per cent of sales in the immediate post-war years - with the bulk going to Latin America. The post-war rise in US exports gradually led to the establishment of sales offices in the principal countries of export. The next stage was the development of local publishing programmes, with the foreign branch offices operating in a dual

137

capacity as export sales agencies and as indigenous publishers. The expansion of McGraw-Hill's international publishing operation accelerated in the 1960s and early 1970s. Table 70 gives a picture of when distribution and publishing of the various stages of development was started in the major subsidiaries. In Canada the acquisition of Ryerson Press in December 1970 greatly added to the scale of the Canadian operations; McGraw-Hill holds 70 per cent of the equity and 30 per cent is in the hands of the public.

The development of a local publishing programme typically starts with translations of US titles, followed by adaptations of these titles, and then the publication of original books by local authors. By 1970 most of the sales of McGraw-Hill International's book operations were generated by titles which were either published or reprinted outside the United States.

Table 70

Distribution and Indigenous Publishing by McGraw-Hill

Country	Start of Distribution	Start of Indigenous Publishing
United Kingdom	1909	1961
Canada	1944	1944
Australia	1964	1964
South Africa	1966	1969
Mexico	1967	1967
Panama	1968	–
West Germany	1969	1971
France	1970	1970
Singapore	1970	–
Brazil	1970	1970
Japan	1972	1974
Colombia	1972	1972
Spain	1973	1981
Portugal	1977	1979

The present position is that McGraw-Hill's International Book Company has operations in seventeen foreign countries and publishes and distributes locally in thirteen languages. There are three sizeable indigenous publishing operations in Canada (where McGraw-Hill Ryerson has a list of over 1,500 Canadian titles in print), the United Kingdom and Australia. The overseas offices whose publishing activity is centred on the translation of US-produced books - but with a leavening of indigenous titles - include Mexico, Brazil, Colombia and French Canada. The other offices remain primarily distribution centres

138

for US exports (and exports of other foreign subsidiaries), but again with often a rising element made up of local publications.

Looking ahead, this pattern of overseas development is likely to persist, with local publishing at least maintaining its position. Inevitably, however, with McGraw-Hill now having a significant presence in most of its major markets, the rate at which new national publishing operations are started will not be sustained. What is to be anticipated is greater breadth being given to the activities of individual subsidiaries. In terms of subject, an area of emphasis will be the development of materials for teaching English throughout the world. Also, with the formation in 1981 of the McGraw-Hill International Training Systems Group (combining Education and Tratec), a concentrated effort at exploiting the multi-media training materials designed for business and industry may be anticipated.

In summary, the extent of the international development of McGraw-Hill is contained in the following statistics: in 1964 some 15 per cent of all the books McGraw-Hill sold abroad were published abroad, in 1974 the proportion was 55 per cent and in 1981 it had risen to approximately 61 per cent.

The chronological sequence leading to the present pattern of Harper & Row (Australia)'s business has a number of surprising features: initially Harper & Row were represented by agents; then they had a joint distribution arrangement with Addison & Wesley, but with separate sales forces. And in 1970, they became a self-contained operation with their own distribution centre. Currently two-thirds of their business is made up of tertiary textbook sales (including the strong Lipincott nursing list) and one-third of general trade publishing. Their sales force consists of six in Australia for tertiary and professional reference, five for trade publishing and one in New Zealand. The New Zealand market has been opened, as is the case with the Australian market, apart from the 15 per cent of titles that account for close to 95 per cent of sales. Harper & Row have, in addition, secured the agencies (normally selling as well as distribution) for Yale, Chicago, MIT, Harvard, Oxmoor Press, West Publishing, D. C. Hulth, Worth and others. A limited amount of local publishing is undertaken, chiefly on the trade side.

The Australian tertiary market is seen as having been 'tied up' some years ago by US firms, in terms of imported and locally published books and this is judged to be irreversible for the foreseeable future. On fundamentals, the next few years will be hampered by indifferent population trends. The possibility of developing any significant export business out of Australia is regarded as remote, at least in the education area.

The purchase, in May 1982, of Cassell Ltd by CBS did not represent a net increase in the US publishing presence in the

UK because the vendor was the US group Macmillan Inc. The reasons for its acquisition are, however, worth mentioning since they help to illustrate the strategy of US majors in international publishing. Having run down the trade publishing side in 1981, Cassell consisted of three imprints:
(a) Cassell specializing in school, business and technical education materials, English as a foreign language, reference books;
(b) Bailliere Tyndall, medical, nursing and veterinary publishers;
(c) Geoffrey Chapman, publisher of religious texts.
Cassell also has the UK trade distribution agency for the Berlitz phrase books and travel guides. In CBS's eyes this purchase served to strengthen the specialist character of its international publishing, which is viewed as the key to future growth. CBS drew particular attention to the good fit of Bailliere, Tyndall with its existing medical imprint Holt-Saunders, and to the fact that they now have a position in English as a foreign language. With McGraw-Hill also emphasizing English language teaching, it could become a crowded field.

Comment

This section has been devoted to trying to obtain a 'feel' for the extent of the American challenge to UK publishers. In now trying to draw the threads together, it should perhaps come as little surprise that the evidence by no means all points in the same direction. If it did, the issue need not have been raised in the first place.

The statistics - whose imperfections must not be overlooked - reveal a sustained rise of 14.1 per cent per annum in US exports - not all that different from the 12.8 per cent rate achieved by UK exports over the same period. However, adjusted for inflation, in real terms US sales abroad have most probably been quite a lot stronger than UK sales abroad.

Turning to individual national markets and particularly to traditional Commonwealth markets, over the whole period US exports to Canada have fallen below the average, those to Australia, New Zealand, West Germany, Holland and the UK have been above average, while exports to Nigeria have exploded. The most consistently above-average growth has been experienced, however, in the 'all other countries' category. In recent years, US exports to South Africa and to New Zealand have been exceptionally strong, a fact that the averages for the full ten-year period mask by reason of the fact that US export growth to those countries in the earlier years was slow.

An analysis of the subject divisions by country throws up the strength of the 'all other' category in the traditional Commonwealth markets. The buoyancy of this residual category represents the interaction of numerous forces, some of which were listed earlier. Attention has already been drawn to the fact that the strongest inroads into traditional UK export markets occurred in the period 1979 to 1981 which coincided with a considerable degree of disarray in the UK industry, together with significant adverse currency movements. Since then UK publishers have regained, for the most part, their poise and at the same time the turnaround in currencies has been reflected in a weakening in the dollar value of US book exports.

If one now moves to the evidence of the case histories, it must be accepted that the sample appears extremely small. The hope is that it is not unrepresentative. Furthermore, it is buttressed by a wide range of additional contacts among both US and UK publishers.

The first point to make is that the US publisher, dedicated to international business of the McGraw-Hill stamp, is in a position of dominance from which he will not readily be dislodged. The type of counter-attack that UK publishers may be able to mount is discussed in the section on the United States. It involves very much more than increasing exports out of the UK on the back of a relative improvement in prices.

A second point is that there is no evidence of any general move among US publishers of non-professional books to attack the UK traditional markets in the aftermath of the Consent Decree. Instead, what emerges is a wide variety of differing approaches to international business. What is certain (and this is borne out by the figures) is that many US publishers found the trend of their exports up to 1981-82 extremely gratifying. And this may well have given them a taste for overseas business and undoubtedly greater experience in the field.

Despite such successes, foreign business for many publishers remains peripheral to their main activity - 5 to 10 per cent of their business perhaps. When circumstances change to their disadvantage they can afford to turn away. They are all the more likely to do so when the cause of their discomfiture is something they do not readily understand and they have no way of influencing, ie currency movements. In this connection, the Mexican devaluation of 1983 was a powerful reminder to US publishers of the heavy risks that international business can carry. It has undoubtedly contributed to the current mood among many US publishers which is pointing them towards a stabilization/diminution of activity abroad rather than an increase.

For UK publishers, this presents an opportunity to try to restore positions that may have been eroded in overseas markets, the urgency of which is increased by the knowledge that economic circumstances and US business opinion can be very volatile. In addition, some UK publishers have taken advantage of the fact that publishing is more genuinely international than it was, and demonstrated that it is possible to marry their UK and Commonwealth strengths to US publishing initiatives.

141

TECHNOLOGY

Pira published in October 1982 a report for the International Electronic Publishing Research Centre entitled Electronic Publishing Technical Scenario: Implications for Book, Newspaper and Periodical Publishers. It ran to 277 pages, and proved to be a clear and fascinating account of the many practical possibilities thrown up by modern technology. Significantly, however, it was light on implications, though it confirmed, for instance, that the novel was unlikely to be produced in electronic versions, whereas dictionaries, encyclopaedias, directories and year books were ideally suited to handling in database form. While this comment certainly does not do justice to the quality of the report, it contains a sufficient number of grains of truth to warrant being retained. It also illustrates the dangers that face anybody who sets out to discuss the effects modern technological developments are likely to have on UK book publishing.

One of the main practical points of relevance to book publishers that emerged from the Pira study was the certain growth that will take place in the use of word processors and computerized methods of handling information, together with the need for publishers to become totally familiar with these techniques. In so doing, they are much more likely to exploit effectively the publishing opportunities that such methods of holding material offer.

In the present chapter, what will be attempted is a brief look at an area which is currently experiencing rapid development and is covered in the report, namely video, and to do so in relation to the consumer market. The subject of video itself breaks down into two, video cassette recorders, the development and exploitation of which is in full swing, and video discs, which are not yet a commercial proposition but may become so in two to three years' time. In addition, the home computer market is touched upon, with particular reference to the links with book publishing.

1. Video Cassette Recording

Industry Background and Projections

The development, in the 1960s, by the Japanese, of portable video tape recorders and small format tape provided the technical advance that has enabled consumer demand for video to develop as it has. The real impetus came in the mid 1970s, as demonstrated in video tape recorder production statistics.

Production is dominated by three manufacturers: JVC's VHS system (70 per cent of the world market), Sony's Betamax system (25 per cent market share) and Philips' V2000 system (5 per

143

cent market share). In September 1981 the number of video tape recorders produced exceeded for the first time the number of colour television sets. For 1983, Screen Digest has estimated a world population of video recorders of around 35m.

Table 71

World Production of Video Tape Recorders

	Year's Production	% Change	Cumulative Growth
(thousand units)			
1977	763		763
1978	1,471	+93	2,234
1979	2,204	+50	4,438
1980	4,441	+102	8,879
1981	9,542	+115	18,421
1982 est.	13,000	+36	31,421

Source: Screen Digest

As is widely recognized, the UK has witnessed explosive growth in demand for video recorders over the last three years, see Table 72. The 1982 purchases represented outlays of some £329m, and by the end of that year 18 per cent of all UK TV homes had a video recorder (see Table 73). The UK is third behind the USA and Japan in video recorder units in use; over 60 per cent of the existing video recorder population in the UK is rented, though a trend is emerging - partly arising from the relaxation of hire purchase restrictions in 1982 - towards an increase in purchases, particularly of the less sophisticated models. Looking ahead, the 3M Company has estimated that the total UK video population would reach 7.7m units in 1985, at which point household penetration would amount to between 35 per cent and 40 per cent. The forecasts made by Media Leisure and shown in Table 73 point to somewhat higher figures for 1985 and suggest that by 1988 household penetration will exceed 50 per cent assuming a video population of 11.6m.

In terms of usage, the evidence so far is that the recording capacity of video is what attracts the consumer most: recent research findings were that 86 per cent of video recorder usage in the UK was for self-recording rather than for viewing rented or purchased programmes.

Of the pre-recorded tapes that are rented or purchased, 54 per cent is made up of feature films, 21 per cent consists of pornography, 8 per cent sport, pop music 5 per cent and the balance of 12 per cent assorted subjects. For the future, with

144

the development of stereo TV and stereo video over the next few years, a safe assumption is that music tapes will become more important. And as the video recorder population expands, the economics of original productions designed for video will improve and the present dependence on material created for films and television stands to diminish.

Table 72

Sales of Video Recorders in the United Kingdom

	Annual Sales	% Change	Cumulative video population
(thousand units)			
1976	15		15
1977	20	+33	35
1978	90	+350	125
1979	175	+94	300
1980	375	+114	675
1981	900	+140	1,575
1982	1,350	+50	2,925
1983 est.	1,800	+33	4,725

Source: 'Media Leisure', Screen Digest, Leisure Consultants

At the present time, there are around 3,000 pre-recorded video cassettes on the market in the UK, of which an estimated one-third derive from four major groups, Warner Communications, Thorn-EMI, CIC (jointly owned by Universal and Paramount) and Twentieth-Century Fox. At the retail end, for every one video cassette sold in the UK, 10½ are rented. Retail multiples are believed to account for some 10 per cent of the business and independent outlets for 90 per cent; the number of dealers increased in two years from 5,000 in 1980 to 15,000 in 1982, of which around 7,000-8,000 were exclusively video shops. This explosive growth has now been followed by a sharp contraction in numbers of outlets, many of which had been inadequately financed. A factor in the decline and fall of video shops - and of the withdrawal of such groups as W. H. Smith and Woolworths from video rental - was undoubtedly the impact of piracy: at one stage illegal copies were estimated to have accounted for up to 70 per cent of all videogram transactions. Since mid-1983, partly as a result of vigorous lobbying, the problem has been checked following an amendment to the Copyright Act under which Magistrates' Courts are entitled to impose heavy fines on retailers offering pirated films for hire or sale.

Video and Book Publishing

A number of UK groups have made significant commitments to video-related publishing, most notably S. Pearson. Longman Video was set up in October 1982 with initial resources of £2m (and a further back-up of £3m). Of the first fifteen launch titles, four were Longman Video originals, including, for children, 'Nursery Rhymes', a mixture of animation, puppets and actors. Other series included 'The Best of World Cinema' and 'International Opera Season'. In December 1982 it was announced that Bookwise would handle the titles in the Longman catalogue exclusively for bookshop sales, leaving CBS distributing to video and record outlets.

Penguin, for their part, reported in January 1983 the setting up of a new imprint 'Penguin Study Video', to specialize in educational video and print packages based on O and A Level English literature texts. The first programme, entitled 'Charles Dickens and Great Expectations', was done in conjunction with the Inner London Education Authority's Television Centre.

Among other publishers that have a video programme, Mitchell Beazley announced in December 1981 a $3m co-production agreement with Thorn-EMI Video Programmes.

In 1983, the periodical and provincial newspaper publishers, East Midland Allied Press, formed EMAP Video, to make programmes directly related to the areas of sports and hobbies covered by their magazines. The first release 'So You Want To Be A Glamour Photographer' involved initial research which established that 70,000 Practical Photography and Camera readers owned or rented a video cassette recorder.

On the distribution front, the decision by Heffer of Cambridge to open a video unit in their main shop attracted a certain amount of attention. Their geographical location puts them, no doubt, in a better position than most to go for quality and thereby avoid the rough and tumble at the lower end of the market. One of the most interesting features was the rationale behind the move as explained by John Welch in a Bookseller article: 'We believe that books and video go together, for we are retailers of knowledge and communication' and again 'We also believe that like TV, video is not an enemy of the book, but complementary: and the same stories and non-fiction subjects recur in both media'.

2. Video Discs and Optical Discs

Video Discs

As summarized in Pira's June 1981 report on video discs, their chief advantages over other media are their ability to store large amounts of information with fast and easy access, their ability to provide quality colour pictures and sound, and their low unit manufacturing costs. When linked with microprocessors or computers, they offer opportunities for the user to interact with the programmed material.

The disc itself is similar in appearance to a record; it needs a special player which is connected to an ordinary television set through the aerial socket. The more costly system involves the use of a laser beam which reads the pits that have been created in the disc; there is clearly no wear and tear on the disc through use. The less expensive alternative is a grooved capacitance system, using a pick-up stylus, which comes into direct contact with the disc. At the present time, it is impossible for the user to record material himself, which sets it apart from the video tape. A major practical advantage that the video disc has over the video tape, however, is that it cannot be pirated easily to make other video discs - though it can doubtless be used as a master in the production of illicit video cassette recordings.

There are three manufacturers who have developed video disc players:
(1) The RCA SelectaVision System (CED), launched in the USA nationally in 1981.
(2) Philips Laser Vision which was first marketed in 1978.
(3) JVC's Very High Density disc (VHD) launched in 1983.
Technical difficulties have bedevilled most of these systems and have been held responsible for the limited impact to date, of what amounts to first generation models.

Optical Discs

The optical disc offers a facility for the mass storage of data for computer systems at low cost. Related peripherals include scanners and hard copy printers, while the system may be connected to word processors for the input of text and to visual display units for information retrieval purposes, all in turn linked on a minicomputer.

So far there are about five commercial products that have been developed, and work is being done by some thirty other companies worldwide.

Markets for Video Discs and Optical Discs

There are three main markets for exploitation, using video and/or optical discs:
(a) the leisure market;
(b) the institutional/industrial market;
(c) the data storage field.
Video discs are primarily involved in the first two and optical discs in the third.

147

Price is expected to play an important role in the spread of video discs since the players themselves are expected to be cheaper than video recorder players and the discs very much less expensive than video tapes. Initially, the public will be offered popular films and television programmes by the equipment manufacturers, but as the player population rises, it will become economic to create special material. This is seen as creating opportunities for joint productions between producers/publishers/television companies/film companies. And in this connection, the suitability of video disc systems for applications in education and training, arising notably out of their interactive capability, will mean that much of the creative work can be expected to be didactic in character. The costs of producing original material for video disc recording are bound to be high, and this will act as a further incentive towards joint production.

An example of a publishing/video disc link concerns Houghton & Mifflin's video disc project, showing birds in their natural habitat and including recordings of their songs, which is a companion to their Field Guide to Birds. More ambitiously, last June Longman and Grolier Inc. revealed plans to develop a video disc encyclopaedia for use as a family reference work. The disc encyclopaedia will contain a mixture of text, newly originated film, library footage, graphic charts, computer generated graphics and archival material. The first disc should be available for sale towards the end of 1984 and subsequent discs will be made available seriatim, in much the same way as a partwork. The second stage of the publishing project will involve the integration of the visually presented data with Grolier's existing on-line database, which will enable the information on the disc encyclopaedia to be updated from the home.

In the area of data storage, major potential markets are in library systems, thereby relieving them of some of the physical storage problems that they have had to contend with. Some observers in the United States envisage the eventual use of video discs in the direct provision of information, whether it be to other libraries or ultimately to customers, leading to a reduction in the demand for books from that source.

Overall projections of the population of video disc players must at this stage be highly problematical. Sales in the United States in 1983 of around 400,000 have been suggested as a reasonable estimate. Following the full commercialization of video discs Philips anticipate that 10 per cent of households will have acquired players within six to eight years, and RCA, that a market penetration of over 30 per cent will have been achieved within ten years. However, the evidence to date indicates that potential demand is greater in commercial applications rather than consumer. An important boost to video discs came with the announcement in January that IBM was ordering from Philips 500 videodisc players which will be used by IBM's dealers to promote its personal computer; the interactive programme which has been developed includes film, slides and animation; it can be overlaid with graphics and text and is being produced in five languages. In another development Thorn EMI is introducing a VHD system in the UK for commercial and industrial use; plans to introduce it as a consumer product have been indefinitely postponed.

3. Home Computers

The home computer boom has been well chronicled. In Table 73 estimates of the home computer population are given through to 1988. By that date household penetration could be close to one third. In the United States, where the penetration is less than in the UK, the current home computer population is put at 5m and is forecast to rise to 50m by 1985; McGraw Hill for their part anticipate that within ten years the number will exceed 100m.

As in the case of video, a number of publishers have entered the software market. In the summer of 1983, Longmans published its first three titles for young children. One title provides an introduction for four to six year-olds to simple addition and subtraction using colourful moving graphics. Another is a pictorial introduction to the alphabet and word recognition. The software is for use on the Sinclair ZX Spectrum. The publishing house of Macmillan is also involved with Sinclair in a range of educational computer software for children. Heinemann has been developing its software interests and a recent spin off, Hill MacGibbon Ltd, is concentrating on software for home computers, with particular emphasis on education for 5 to 16 year-olds. To take another example in the UK, Pan Books has plans to enter the software market in 1984 covering both software only (in tape or disc) and software with tie-in titles. While in the United States, computer software is entering publishers' lists with ever increasing frequency.

Preceding this gradual move into computer software publishing has been the explosion in the publication of computer books and computer magazines on both sides of the Atlantic. Indeed this is an instance of the dynamic effects on book and periodical publishing that a piece of electronic hardware can have and one that is competing directly with print for the consumer's money and leisure. Part of the strength of trade paperbacks in the USA is attributable to the vigorous sales of computer books, which often appear in that format. In the UK, computer books have not yet received the accolade of a separate entry in The Bookseller's list of titles, so that books on programming are included under mathematics, hardware under engineering, software under general and business under commerce. The launch of computer book lists by publishers is an almost weekly occurrence and there is no questioning the current boom conditions.

4. Projections

If one turns to the video and computer projections in the following table, the intriguing consideration is that while the rate of installation of units is bound to fall, growth in demand for products to put into this expanding population of machines should be well sustained. This is precisely the market to which book publishers can contribute most.

Table 73

Projections for UK Video and Home Computer Installations

	1982	1983	1984	1985	1988
Television					
Household penetration	97%	98%	98%	98%	99%
of which colour	77%	80%	82%	83%	85%
Video Cassette Recorders					
VCR's (m units)	3.8	5.8	7.0	8.0	11.6
Household penetration	18%	28%	33%	37%	53%
Home Computers					
Computers (m units)	1.0	2.2	3.4	4.4	7.0
Household penetration	5%	11%	16%	21%	32%

Source: Leisure Forecasts, Media Leisure, Leisure Consultants, September 1983

SUMMARIES AND CONCLUSIONS

1. World Population Environment

Among developing countries population will expand by 776m in the 1980s, against 649m in the 1970s, the fastest growth occurring in Latin America and Africa.

Among developed countries, the population increase in the 1980s of 85m will fall short of the 89m advance in the 1970s. There will also be an actual contraction of 5m in the 0-24-year-old band. The implications are, broadly, unhelpful for those supplying the educational market.

Within the UK, in contrast to the overall experience of developed countries, population growth will be greater in the 1980s than it was in the 1970s, with the contrast being particularly marked in respect of the period of static population between 1976 and 1981. The educational band (0-19) will, however, experience an actual contraction. Against this, the number aged between 20 and 44 will rise by 2m, or a good 10 per cent; in relation to book buying habits, this should (ceteris paribus) be positive for book publishing.

In the United States population expansion in the 1980s will be at the same rate as in the 1970s. The educational band will suffer a fractional fall, population growth being concentrated, as in the United Kingdom, in the 22-44-year-old bracket.

In Australia the population will rise at a compound rate of 1.5 per cent, the same as in the 1970s. While some growth will occur in the 0-19 band, most of the advance will be concentrated in the adult population.

In the UK, USA and Australia, three of the most important markets for UK publishers, demographic developments in the 1980s will act as a stimulus to economic activity. More generally, those publishers who satisfy the leisure and instructional needs of the working population will be the principal beneficaries of such trends.

2. Economic Environment

The 1970s had to cope with the two major oil shocks, in 1973 and 1979, which led to a massive transfer of wealth from the non-oil producing countries to the oil producing countries. This had both a depressing effect on world economic activity, and a stimulating effect on world inflation. Third World non-oil producers were particularly exposed, since they were not able to respond by expanding their exports to the oil producers as did many of the industrialized countries.

The surplus capacity that now exists in crude oil production, allied to the continuing effects on oil demand of energy conservation measures among the industrialized countries, should enable any pick-up in consumption arising out of an increase in economic activity to be satisfied without causing renewed upward pressures on prices. Indeed in the shorter term, some possibility exists of prices actually being reduced. Always assuming the absence of political developments in the Middle East that could readily falsify these suggestions, the next few years look like being relatively less favourable for Third World oil producers and relatively more favourable for non-oil producers.

If one also takes into account the fact that many politicians now recognize that there are few advantages for them to be seen to be presiding over rising prices, the political will is present, to a much greater extent than previously, for holding down inflation. We could well be at the start of a period of several years when inflation will remain under generally good control at relatively low levels. Such an environment would mean that economic growth would be healthy, that is to say not leading inevitably to the economic pressures that have bedevilled the last ten years, and permitting a significant reduction in interest rates.

One of the more tantalizing prospects is, in fact, a cyclical upturn in world economic activity associated with the dismantling of the defences needed to give protection from an inflation rate that at one time had got out of control. This would also hold out the promise of an extended period of economic recovery, since the upturn would be stretched out through the delayed appearance of those distortions and bottlenecks that are associated with inflationary growth.

A situation of comparatively stable inflation would prove favourable for publishing. While some industries have been clear inflation beneficiaries - notably those that have enjoyed inflationary stock profits and escalating values of fixed assets - this has not been the case with publishing. For publishing does not create inventory profits and, with most of its capital tied up in stock and work in progress, has generally failed to participate in rising asset values. And then there has been the burden of financing these short-term assets at a time when high inflation rates have been characterized by high interest rates.

3. Trends in the Demand for Books

Over the past ten years, demand for books as reflected in the sales of the publishing industries of developed countries has led to sizeable sales increases by value. Adjusted for inflation, however, in recent years there has been little or no growth, the worst experience being that of the UK, where the figures point to an actual drop in sales in real terms since 1980, whereas in Australia and the United States real sales have done little more than hold steady.

Such findings are certainly too gloomy, one reason being that the analysis does not go beyond the year 1982, which saw the trough of the worst post-war recession suffered by the industrialized nations. Secondly, the evidence itself is not clear cut, given the statistical shortcomings that seem to be a feature of publishing throughout the world. In the UK, three methods exist for adjusting for inflation; all of them are open to criticism and each gives a reading that is different to the others. Indeed, in the UK other evidence such as consumer outlays on books suggest that during the 1970s books successfully maintained their share of expanding consumer expenditure in real terms (and raised their share in value terms). Furthermore they appear to have done this despite powerful rival claims on consumer discretionary income.

Looking ahead, the cyclical upturn that started in 1983 will have corrected in that year much of the downward distortion to which the 1982 figures were subject. Providing the economic recovery is sustained, one can anticipate that the improvement in consumer spending on books will be gradually extended to the institutional markets which have been depressed in all three countries; they are typically laggards in the cycle since their funding is tied to government revenues, notably tax receipts.

Beyond the near term, the latest edition of the Henley Centre for Forecasting's 'Leisure Features' suggests that UK book sales in constant price terms will fluctuate around what is a horizontal line through to 1988. On the other hand, in Australia, continued population expansion and the stimulus provided by the bi-centenary celebrations in 1988 should lead to an element of real growth. While in the United States, the latest Book Industry Study Group projections suggest a rate of increase in book sales of a thoroughly respectable 7 per cent. This compares favourably with growth in the five years from 1977 to the recession year of 1982 of 12 per cent by value and 3.1 per cent in units.

Longer term, for confidence to be expressed in a sustained increase in book demand, a number of uncomfortable considerations have to be faced. Most fundamental of all concerns the habit of reading. As Martyn Goff director of the National Book League has frequently deplored, children read less and less and this clearly has ominous implications for future book demand. Moreover, other calls on the public's disposable income and leisure seem set to grow further and most probably at a rate that will exceed that of rising earnings and increasing free time. A persuasive argument is that videos, home computers, etc. do indeed pose a more serious challenge than was the case with some of the 'new' products developed in the 1960s and 1970s, ie the switch from black and white to colour television, the growth of travel and the blossoming of new tastes in food and drink. One big change is that whereas TV came free (barring the set), video cassettes, video games, cable have to paid for. At the same time, it seems quite possible that the development of cable television in the UK will be much slower than the American experience might have led one to believe.

The balance of opinion, as illustrated in the predictions of the Henley Centre and some other forecasting groups, is that one should not anticipate much real growth over the medium to longer term in consumer demand for books. And in the area of information and instruction, it seems clear that the commitment to the book as the means of communication stands to be reduced. An extreme expression of this view comes from F. W. Lancaster, University of Illinois: 'Whether we like it or not, print will eventually give way completely to electronics, at least for those publications designed primarily to transmit factual information rather than to entertain'[1].

While the publishing role of selecting and moulding what is to be disseminated remains unchanged, the range of methods that can be used to transmit to the intended audience the material that has been chosen has been greatly expanded. This translates into additional calls on the publisher's imagination and initiative, and constitutes as well a financial challenge.

To date, the response of many book publishers has been far from passive. In the consumer market, the plethora of computer books, tied in to the boom in home computer ownership is an encouraging example of how a possible threat to the book has been turned to advantage. More directly, a firm such as Longman, whose chief executive Tim Rix has for many years been a vigorous exponent of combining traditional and modern methods of communication in education, is investing sizeable sums in software programmes for video and home computers. Moreover, as the novelty goes out of these products, it can be expected that they will be less used purely for entertainment (games) and more for practical purposes (domestic programmes) and home instruction. These are areas where the publisher's expertise is called into play.

4. Changes in Format

A major post-war development in English language publishing relates to format and is epitomized in the term 'the paperback revolution'. To take one set of statistics, US publishers' sales of adult trade books in 1963 were 13 per cent paperback and 87 per cent hardback, and in 1982 the percentages were 32 per cent paperback and 68 per cent hardback. Such figures do not, however, give a complete picture of the swing to paperback format, since they fail to cover the expansion of limp cover educational books and the growing acceptance by the institutiional market of paperback format books that do not fall under the mass-market label. More subtly, perhaps, the prejudice in the minds of consumers that paperback meant cheap, but probably

[1] Quoted in Book Libraries and Electronics, Knowledge Industry Publications, 1982

nasty, has largely been dispelled, while in the younger generation it is often replaced by an almost proprietorial attitude
to paperbacks as 'their kind of book'. Another feature of the
paperback scene in the USA - and increasingly in the UK - is
the burgeoning of the trade paperback sold primarily through
traditional book outlets and produced in very much smaller
quantities than is typical of mass-market titles. An analysis
of the trade paperback market in the USA concluded that trade
paperbacks formed the fastest growing, and therefore, the most
exciting area of publishing.

It has now become virtually impossible for any sizeable
publisher not to be heavily involved in paperbacks. If the
disparity in rates of growth persists between the two formats -
in 1987 43 per cent of the US adult trade books may be paperbacks (see Table 61) - the time must be approaching when
paperbacks will overtake hardbacks in several areas of
publishing. This has implications in terms of structure, both
at the industrial and at the company levels, through the breakdown of many of the traditional divisions between the different
formats. Examples taken from UK publishing houses where this is
occurring and which have been commented upon here include
Associated Book Publishers, Penguin, Viking Penguin and Faber
& Faber.

5. UK Distribution

In UK book distribution, considerable reliance will continue to
be placed on existing outlets. In this connection W. H. Smith
and Menzies will retain their importance and their declared
intention of developing further their book interests is an
encouraging pointer to the future. The stock holding bookseller
will also continue to have a crucial role to play. The evidence
of poor profitability among Charter booksellers is, however,
worrying, leading as it does in an increasing number of cases
to bookshops being unable to maintain their traditional position in the high street. Against this the growth of book
chains, and the ambitious expansion plans of some groups into
bookselling, indicate optimism on the score of bookshop
profitability. An intriguing situation relates to the CTNs and
the variety store chains. It is recognized that in the UK mass-
market paperbacks may not resume their previous rates of
growth; under the influences discussed earlier, the underlying
trend of mass-market sales seems unlikely to do more than sta-
bilize at lower levels. However, the progressive establishment
of small book departments, encompassing a broader range of
titles, as the average CTN unit becomes larger, opens up other
opportunities for book sales in such outlets. Recognition by an
increasing number of British retail chains that books can offer
attractive margins is one of the reasons for the growth in the
UK of a firm such as Octopus. It also provides an encouraging

framework within which a number of UK trade book publishers can develop their general lists.

Book publishing has seen a burgeoning of special interest publishing. The subject lists bear testimony to the diversity that exists and illustrate where activity has proved greatest over the last ten years. The expansion of trade paperbacks is also a direct reflection of the demand for books sold at a 'reasonable' price whose appeal is not sufficiently wide to justify mass-market treatment. There is every indication that this whole area remains one of further expansion. In terms of retailing, such a trend lends support to the development of the more traditional book outlets. It could also encourage publishers to strengthen their direct sales capabilities.

6. Overseas Developments

The declining proportion of UK book exports as a percentage of total publishers' sales is well documented. How much of that is to be explained by a fall in the competitiveness of UK books abroad and how much by the replacement of exports by indigenous overseas publishing on the part of UK firms cannot be established with any precision. Part at least of the deterioration in the period between 1978 and 1982 (which saw exports as a percentage of the total decline from 36.6 per cent to 30.5 per cent) must be laid at the door of decreasing competitiveness, coinciding as it did with an escalating exchange rate. The effects moreover persisted into the period when the overvaluation of sterling began to be corrected.

At the same time as sterling was rising, the dollar was falling and this found its counterpart in sustained growth in US book exports. It also gave rise to the fear within the UK trade that the United States publishing industry had undergone a sea change in its approach to overseas markets in the aftermath of the breakdown of the traditional UK market agreement.

US competition in markets outside the USA is consistently powerful in an area such as tertiary education (where the USA has a dominant position) and intermittently so in mass-market paperbacks (where American publishers take advantage of any sharp improvements that occur in their price competitiveness). The evidence does not point, however, to any fundamental shift in the American industry's attitude to international sales. A willingness to seize in an opportunistic way on an improvement in trading terms is evident, as is a sharp cooling of enthusiasm once these terms start moving against them.

This leaves the British based publisher in a position that does not appear to have altered in practice all that significantly from the period preceding the Consent Decree. More positively, it has spurred some firms to capitalize on the traditional strengths that they enjoy. The arrangements between Simon & Schuster and Hodder & Stoughton over the marketing of the Silhouette romance imprint in Britain and Australia is a case in point. The wide-spread international links being established between Avon Books and Bantam's UK subsidiary, Corgi, is another such instance.

Indigenous publishing is a theme that has run through much of this report and its successful development undoubtedly goes some way towards explaining the fall in the proportion of UK publishers' sales accounted for by exports. In Australia, the transformation of that market from purely an export outlet for UK titles to increasingly a centre of indigenous publishing is clear cut. This trend has been particularly pronounced in the educational field. For the future, the emphasis on local publishing can be expected to continue, which will mean a growing editorial investment by British houses in their Australian subsidiaries if they wish to maintain their positions in that market.

Of more recent date is the successful establishment of a publishing presence in the USA by a number of UK houses. In some instancess this is seen as a logical extension of existing interests: Associated Book Publishers with their scientific lists, Longman in English/American language teaching and in medicine, Routledge & Kegan Paul in academic publishing. In other cases, the growth prospects of the American market which are seen to be higher than many others, acts as the chief magnet. This is partly behind Penguin's substantial commitment to the US market through Viking Penguin, and is the motivation for the major investments made by International Thomson Organisation in professional and business publishing.

Finally, on a very much more modest scale a number of other UK publishers are seeking to strengthen their selling arrangements in the US market often edging towards some form of direct representation.

The characteristic that the American market used to have of a graveyard for UK publishing ambitions has not deserted it completely, as the experiences of W. H. Smith and William Collins bear witness. However the spirit, if such it was, is being exorcised and a move towards more direct exposure for UK publishers in the US market is now established and seems likely to be maintained.

7. UK Publishing

UK publishers will be operating in a worldwide industry characterized by slow underlying real growth during the 1980s. This reflects indifferent population figures in the educational age brackets and rival claims on the discretionary income of consumers. But the position of the UK industry itself has improved significantly.

(a) The commercial overvaluation of sterling, thanks to its petro-currency characteristics, has been corrected in

157

respect of the dollar and some adjustment has occurred in relation to other currencies.

(b) An international environment of low inflation rates is of great assistance to all publishing industries - but none more so than that of the UK, which has had to live with rates of inflation that were well above average.

(c) While underlying real growth rates may be low, a cyclical upturn in economic activity in many industrialized countries is under way.

(d) The breakdown of the British traditional market agreement has not deprived the British publishers of their traditional markets, nor has it devalued their international expertise.

(e) UK publishing has emerged from the recession greatly strengthened by the stringent measures that were forced on it. These have given it much tighter organizations with greater commercial keenness. Management had also learned skills that it had previously not been called upon to excercise, one specific instance being international print buying.

(f) A more questioning attitude to traditional practices also makes it likely that companies will respond to changing developments more swiftly than was previously the case.

(g) This provides a framework within which company profitability can increase even without any marked support from the underlying trends in the industry.

In short, opportunities exist for British publishers, notwithstanding the withdrawal some years ago of a 'growth' label from the Business of Books.